CUP of WONDER

BREAD of LIFE

The Sacrament of
Holy Communion

CUP *of* WONDER

BREAD *of* LIFE

The Sacrament of Holy Communion

Martin Recio

WINEPRESS  PUBLISHING

Printed in the United States of America

Packaged by WinePress Publishing, PO Box 428, Enumclaw, WA 98022. The views expressed or implied in this work reflect those of the author. The author(s) is ultimately responsible for the design, content, and editorial accuracy of this work.

Scripture references are taken from the King James Version of the Bible, unless otherwise noted.

Verses marked RSV are taken from the Revised Standard Version of the Bible. Copyright 1946, 1952, 1971 by the Division of Christian Education of the National Council of the Churches of Christ in the U.S.A. Used by permission.

ISBN 1-57921-399-5
Library of Congress Catalog Card Number: 2001093581

CONTENTS

PREFACE

Our Lord held the Last Supper on the night of the Passover feast. Jesus took his form for the sacrament of Holy Communion from this meal. The Passover meal commemorated the redemption of Israel from bondage in Egypt, on the night when the blood of the lamb slain shielded the household from the death of the firstborn, when Israel was created as a nation, and when God fulfilled his promise of deliverance. Each one of these points—the Passover meal as a whole, the Paschal lamb that was slain, the first-born redeemed by the blood, the deliverance of the people, and the creation of Israel as a nation—may be emphasized separately or together with another point, at different times.

This work is a many-faceted perspective on the sacrament of Holy Communion. We can approach a teaching of our faith (in this instance, the sacrament of Holy Communion) from different avenues, bring out different points of emphasis, and make different applications. This work was planned as an aid in teaching insights on the topic. I have presented twenty approaches that may give an enhanced view on the celebration of the sacrament. My objectives are to open up concepts, stimulate the mind, and expose the theme to greater possibilities. I endeavored to make the work inspirational and beneficial to the spiritual life. I trust that in the application, the sacrament will be found to have spoken to our hearts, souls, and minds. Each chapter is complete in itself, and the work moves progressively to a climax.

FOREWORD

In *Cup of Wonder and Bread of Life*, Martin Recio presents a series of devotional, sermonic essays exploring the various facets of the gem God has given the church in holy communion. Recio includes—yet goes well beyond—the oft discussed facets even as he remains thoroughly anchored in Scripture and orthodox Christianity particularly from a reformed perspective. He shows how the upper room discourses provide a context for the institution of holy communion enriching our understanding. He also explores the implications of placing its institution as an integral part of the climactic phase of Jesus' ministry—the arrest, trial, death, resurrection and exaltation. Emerging from the essays are mature insights borne of a lifetime of pastoral experience, Biblical study, prayerful reflection and informed Christian living. These essays will provoke much thought and result in a deeper understanding of the feast to which our Lord has invited each of us.

Dr. Ernest E. Ettlich
Professor of Rhetoric
Southern Oregon State University
Ashland, Oregon

THE SACRAMENT AND THE WORD

I n the military forces of ancient Rome, within the "legion," a Roman soldier took an oath pledging to obey his commander and not to desert his standard. This oath was called a *sacrament* and was interpreted as a ceremony involving an obligation.

The Sacrament

A sacrament of the Church is a religious ceremony, with sacred and spiritual implications. Traditionally, a sacrament has been defined as an overt, visible sign of inward and spiritual grace. It is a good definition. As a means of grace, a sacrament has divine approval, and it imparts spiritual growth, strength, and blessing. It has redemptive significance. It is also a sign and seal of our relationship with Christ and his Church. A sacrament may also be said to have been instituted by Christ, engaged in by Christ, and approved by him as a means of grace and spiritual blessing. The sacrament works the grace of God in us and imparts encouragement in our religious life. As a religious ceremony, the sacrament involves a response from us. It implies our union with Christ, our worship of him, and our rededication to his kingdom of peace and righteousness. We respond with faith and trust.

Holy Communion

Holy Communion imparts redemptive significance. As a means of grace it effectuates the love of God. It is both a memorial and a testimony to our Savior's love and sacrifice and much more. In Holy Communion, the Presence is encountered, and our spiritual life is renewed and kept strong. Our Lord promised the Church his presence and power. We sense and believe in our Lord's spiritual presence during this sacred ceremony. In this sacrament, we believe that our Lord's presence is more acute than on any other service or ministry of the Church.

The question has arisen: does the bread and wine become more than the mere symbols of our Lord's body and blood? We believe so. The Church doctrine of the Immanence of God applies to all persons of the Trinity. As God is, so also is our Lord Christ Jesus, and so also is the Holy Spirit; they are actively manifested in a living and operative presence throughout the universe. In Holy Communion, that operative presence is a manifestation of redemptive grace: the Holy Spirit applies the grace of our Lord Jesus Christ to all that partake of the consecrated bread and wine. The presence of Christ can be felt in our hearts, sensed in our souls, and acknowledged in our minds.

The bread and wine are more than mere symbols, and the sacrament of Holy Communion is more than a mere memorial. It is also a living, active, spiritual encounter with our risen and living Lord. It is that moment of spirit and truth in which we receive grace for grace and when our Lord comes to us with all his redemptive love and spiritual power. If we apply our intellect just a little, we are led to acknowledge that a mere symbol, by itself, can never be an outpouring of redemptive, spiritual grace. Symbols move us and awaken images of spiritual realities in our minds, but they work no transport of spiritual grace. A transport of spiritual grace is the work of the Holy Spirit. The Holy Spirit awakens our spiritual heart and applies the reality of the Presence to our lives. In spirit and in truth, our Lord is present in the consecrated bread and wine.

When we come to the sacrament, we come amidst holy things; we come into the presence of our Lord's body that was broken for us, and into the presence of his blood that was shed for the remission of sins. As the Spirit calls us, and as our hearts would lead us, we come into our Redeemer's presence with absolute trust and with faith unfeigned. We come seeking, as of old, the Bread of Heaven. Like the heavy laden, we come seeking rest for our souls and peace for our hearts, for here the weary be at rest. We come to feel our spirits uplifted by the grace of renewal and regeneration. We are made aware that together we stand in the presence of a great body of unseen witnesses. We come to embrace the reality of our faith and to acknowledge that our life is hid of God in Jesus Christ. Because of God's grace, this is true in spite of all our faults, failures, and sins. Christ our Lord, he only has covered us over with his righteousness, through the atonement of his cross.

As a Jewel Is Turned

As we turn a jewel to view its many facets, so we will do to the sacrament of Holy Communion. Like searching out the many facets of a precious gem, we will look for its many points of light. True, we will not uncover all the treasures of Holy Communion, but we will deal with those that come most readily to mind. We will look at it as a memorial of our Savior's sacrifice, remembering that our Lord said, "Do this in remembrance of me" (1 Cor. 11:24). We will view Holy Communion as that hour of personal encounter with our Lord, where we come to be refreshed by his grace, and where our souls are restored to the joy of his salvation. We will think of coming to Holy Communion to be strengthened in our faith once more. Again, we will view our coming to Holy Communion as our approach to the sacred altar, where our souls are plunged beneath the cleansing flood and cleansed from all unrighteousness. We will think of coming to Holy Communion seeking him in whom we have been redeemed and who has covered us over with his grace.

We will look at our celebration of Holy Communion as coming to seek absolution by the blood that was shed for the remission of sins and by the body that was given for the life of the world. We will also note that bright facet of Holy Communion that is the summary of the Gospel: how that Christ died for our sins according to the Scriptures, and that he rose again on the third day according to the Scriptures. We come to Holy Communion to show that we bear witness to his death, until our great God and Savior, the Lord Jesus Christ, comes in his Second Advent. And as we view Holy Communion as a testimony of our Savior's death and resurrection, the sacrament of Holy Communion is also a reminder of our hope of immortality. And still, the riches of our Savior's grace and the facets in Holy Communion are unsearchable.

The Sacrament: Ever Old, Ever New

In the sacrament of Holy Communion, we stand in the presence of the Father of our spirits and in the presence of Christ. We unite, all one body we, in worship amidst these elements of bread and wine as have all who have ever walked in the way of the Lord in every generation. In so coming, we discover once again that God's mercy is new every morning. Once again, through our strengthening and renewal, the grace, which is ever old and ever new, reveals itself to us, and our Lord will also reveal himself to us.

Occasionally, we may see and know him as he is, but mostly, God reveals himself through the affections of our minds and the moving of our souls. Thus, we come to the bread and wine to be touched by God, to be in a heartfelt fellowship with him in a true spiritual sense. The hour of Holy Communion, if you desire it and if you seek it, can be that old-and-ever-new religious experience for you personally. You may leave the hour of worship with a new vision of the Most High impressed on your heart and mind. And you will know it, because you have felt it, sensed it, and acknowledged it, and because he who has redeemed your soul from destruction will meet you in the Bread of His Presence. And if you do seek his kingdom and his righteousness first, then at times, his love will simply overwhelm you. And there will be peace, faith, hope, and joy in the Holy Spirit.

The Sacrament and the Word

We come to the hour of worship to be renewed by the sacrament and by the Word of the living God. It is through the Word of God that we understand that his grace and kindness are what give us life, certainty, and peace. Through the Word, we understand that by faith in the Lord Jesus, his grace can transform the whole of an individual life. We are of an age that must be told that faith in Christ is also faith in the Word of the Lord and in his redeeming work. A living faith is also trust in the truth of God as manifested in the life and work of Jesus Christ.

In the sacrament of Holy Communion, in which we remember his sacrifice for us, we come to the "awakening and to the enlightenment" (Justin Martyr), that our faith is to believe in God. In partaking of the bread and wine, it is the redemptive reality of the cross of Christ that we apply to our souls. Having been fed with the Bread of Heaven and the Word, we confess that the Son of God became incarnate, was crucified, and raised again for our salvation, and all according to the word of the Lord.

In coming to the sacrament of Holy Communion, you may personally know Christ and the power of his resurrection. With the sacrament and the Word, your soul is fed, to nourish it and to have it touched by the grace of God, that you may be set free from selfishness and sin. This occurs to all that believe the Word and partake of the sacrament. And once again, we note the wonder and marvel, the simplicity of our faith, which incorporates us with Christ our Lord.

In the quietness and confidence of the hour of worship, amidst the consecrated creatures of bread and wine, the Spirit works his grace. Our souls are sanctified, imbued with trust, rest, and peace. And through it all, we confess with gratitude and in awe and wonder that the faith that I possess, and the trust that you possess, is given us by God the Father. Whenever we partake of Holy Communion, in that mysterious working of God's curious design, our faith is continually fed and kept strong by the sacrament and the Word.

2

THE PASSOVER OF GOD

A s we view Holy Communion in its sacramental significance, we entertain the widest possible perspective. Among other reasons, we gather before the bread and wine of Holy Communion because this service brings to our minds the fulfillment of the Christian promise, the reality of God's love. The words from the Gospel of St. Matthew, spoken by Jesus in the Upper Room, are familiar to us:

> And as they were eating, Jesus took the bread, and blessed it, and brake it, and gave it to the disciples, and said, Take, eat; this is my body. And he took the cup, and gave thanks, and gave it to them, saying Drink ye all of it; For this is my blood of the new testament, which is shed for many for the remission of sins. (Matt. 26:26–29)

The time for these twelve men in that Upper Room of long ago had grown late. The day was far spent and the night had fallen, and the darkness was about to fall on their souls. Their Master was to be taken from them, and they would be left without his physical presence and leadership. The opposition to the Way had drawn to a head, and the hostility of the religious authorities would inflame the mob of the chief priest to madness. The Son of Man was to die at the hands of sinful men. The disciples were anxious, hesitant, and fearful. If ever a group of men needed consolation, this was that group. A hostile world awaited them outside. But here, amidst the elements of bread and wine, Jesus would give them peace, strength, and confidence. He blessed them, consecrated them to holy service, and prayed for them.

Were it not for the ills that affect our human nature, driving us to seek its comfort time and time again, the sacrament might lose its significance. It comes to us like the bush aglow that appeared to Moses, indicating the presence of God. As the spiritual reality of the incarnation of God in Jesus Christ, this sacrament is the most priceless treasure the Church gives to its people.

The Assurance of God's Reception

The grace revealed in Holy Communion is that it assures us of God's reception and forgiveness, symbolizing the Savior's blood, shed for many for the remission of sins. The grace is this: that wherever we may be, at home, at work, on vacation, on a hospital bed, or even in prison, our Savior is quite capable of receiving us. When Paul and Silas had been thrown into the inner cell of the prison in Philippi, something wonderful occurred. God effected their release. Thinking that his prisoners had escaped, the Philippian jailer would have taken his own life. This was a Roman prison and the escape of the prisoners resulted in the forfeit of the jailer's life. St. Paul, aware of the situation, said, "We are all here. Do thyself no harm." Right then and there, in that damp prison cell, the Philippian jailer fell on his knees and asked, "Sirs, what must I do to be saved?" Paul made him the offer of God's reception. He said, "Believe on the Lord Jesus Christ." (Acts 16:31). Anywhere in the world, in the vast regions of interstellar space, or across the fields, the place makes no difference. When a human soul chooses to come to Christ Jesus, that soul can be certain of reception.

One day the lawyers brought to Jesus a woman taken in adultery. They wanted Jesus to judge and condemn her, but the Master saw through their subterfuge. Instead, he drove them all away and received this poor woman. Though she may not have been much in the eyes of the lawyers, Jesus thought otherwise. Lost she may have been, but who has never been lost? Fallen from grace, perhaps. Still, she was a child of God and of more value than many sparrows. Her soul was of infinite worth. She was of value to Jesus Christ. Who can possibly estimate the worth of another individual soul? Not one of us, surely. Besides all that, God is no respector of persons. Whoever, wherever a person chooses to approach the sacrament of Holy Communion, that individual is confirmed in reception by Jesus Christ. To be confident of God's reception is a wonderful thing. We want and need it very much. We have that assurance in Holy Communion.

The Assurance of God's Blessing

Holy Communion brings to memory the reality of God's blessings. The blessings of God are not idle dreams, nor are they the products of wishful thinking. They are a definite, concrete reality. The prophet Isaiah wrote:

> Thus saith the Lord who made thee, and formed thee from the womb, which will help thee: Fear not . . . For I will pour water upon him that is thirsty . . . and . . . upon the dry ground. I will pour my spirit upon thy descendants, and my blessings on your offsprings. (Is. 44:2–3)

The certitude of God's blessing, "Fear not, I am with thee," is sufficient to remove most of our anxieties. Anxiety is worry. It is being troubled over what might happen. Those twelve men in the Upper Room were rather anxious. They were going to be greatly disturbed after the crucifixion. They were a worried and confused fellowship in that Upper Room. Our Lord knew that they would not amount to much or accomplish much if they remained anxious. Jesus applied the knowledge of God's blessing to their hearts in order that through faith in his promise he might remove their anxieties. Our Lord promised them his peace, power, and presence.

Our anxieties can be just as many and just as real as those that troubled the disciples at that hour. There are troubled souls the world over. Thus, it is that when we come to the sacrament of Holy Communion, our Lord offers himself to us again. This is the reminder of the fulfillment of the promise that can drive away anxiety. Were not the disciples afraid when the soldiers came to take Jesus away? Mark was so frightened that he fled from the scene, leaving his cloak in the hands of one of the soldiers. Peter's fear caused him to follow Jesus from a safe distance. There is nothing that can cripple an individual as effectively as fear. Fear can paralyze his actions and even cause him to do the wrong thing. Fear is as real as hands and feet, and the disciples would need a great deal of confidence to overcome their fears. The certitude of God's blessings that our Lord gave to them during that first Holy Communion would help remove those fears. "Fear not," said the Lord, "I will be with thee."

> When thou passest through the waters, I will be with thee; and through the rivers, they shall not overflow thee: when thou walkest through the fire, thou shalt not be burned; neither shall the flame kindle upon thee. (Is. 43:2)

Anxiety, fear, worry, all these can come upon us at one time or another. They are inherent in human nature and we need to be reminded that faith drives away fear. To be removed from fear is a blessing. Yet those who worship here receive much more than this. For while our faith removes fear and anxiety, it also renews courage. Courage is that quality of mind and spirit that enables one to meet the hardships and dangers of life with fortitude. Amidst the doubts and uncertainty of our age, the wars and rumors of wars, and the sagging moral standards, it takes courage to endeavor to be Christ-like, to be long-suffering and warm, to be without guile, and to go on loving an unlovely world.

The Savior had to face the cross, and so would Peter, and the other disciples would suffer hardships. Their courage would have to be renewed day by day if need be. Bringing us to the reality of God's blessing and presence, the holy sacrament can serve to renew courage. While the Christian faith has endured because its quality of love has lived in the hearts of its people, the courage that our faith generated in the lives of its people has enabled them to blaze a path through history of good and noble endeavors.

The Assurance of Immortality
Sharing in our Lord's table, we not only receive confirmation of our reception, but we also obtain a pledge of tomorrow. We are given our token of immortality. As often as we eat this bread and drink this cup, we witness to our oneness in Christ. Because he lives, we too shall live. For as many as have put on Christ Jesus, have put on immortality. This quality of our faith comes through our union with Christ and our being a part of his Church. About this table our mutual fellowship is confirmed. Our fellowship is with the Father and with his Son Jesus Christ, who manifested eternal life. St. John wrote, "And this is the testimony, that God gave us eternal life, and this life is in his Son. He that hath the Son has life" (1 John 5:11–12). There is nothing that can lift our thoughts or elevate our spirits as can the conviction that one day we shall stand in the presence of God with our Redeemer, Jesus Christ. Time will vanish away like a shadow, mortality shall be swallowed up in life, and this mortal shall have put on immortality. We have the reality of this promise in our union and communion with Christ "who brought life and immortality to light" (2 Tim. 1:10).

We know that it is not always easy to believe in things that are unseen or in things that are beyond our immediate experience. At times it is just as difficult for us to believe in the visions and promises of God as it was for some of the Old Testament heroes. God made the promise to Gideon that he would deliver his people from oppression. But Gideon had never been numbered among the mighty men of valor. How could he who hid in the fields from the enemy ever deliver his people from oppression? Gideon wanted a sign, a symbol, an indication that God had really spoken and that it was not all an idle dream. He put out the fleece to be wet one day and dry the next. God responded, giving Gideon the confirmation that the Eternal had spoken. The holy sacrament is a sign, a symbol, and a pledge of God's faithfulness to us. It brings to us a better reality and confirmation than any Old Testament sign. That reality is the nourishment of our souls through the bread and wine of Christ. Only the things of the Spirit can quicken our souls and make us feel and sense the presence of the eternal and cause us to embrace the promise of immortality. Spiritual realities make us aware of the love of God. Ultimately, we must rest our all on the non-discursive side of our being. It is here that God would move us to the assurance of things unseen.

The Passover of God

Knowing that his hour had come, the Lord Jesus desired to eat the Paschal supper with his disciples. Instructed by their Master, the disciples found an obscure Upper Room and made preparation for the Passover Meal. On the night of the Passover Meal, our Lord instituted the sacrament of Holy Communion. He took the form of the Passover Meal and transformed it into the bread and wine of Holy Communion, full and running over with the spiritual realities of his Gospel.

The Passover commemorated the redemption of Israel from bondage. On the night of Israel's redemption, a Paschal lamb was slain, and its blood sprinkled on the two side-posts and the upper doorpost of the home. The blood of the lamb slain shielded the household from the death of the firstborn when the Lord God passed through to smite the Egyptians. God would "pass over the door," so that it would not be granted the destroyer to enter their dwelling. Although Israel was created as a nation on the night of the Passover, the emphasis is on Israel's redemption from bondage. The Paschal lamb is symbolic of our Lord's sacrifice, where on the cross, the Lord Jesus wrought the redemption of his people.

This is the main significance of the sacrament of Holy Communion.

We are aware that bread and wine are common elements, the stuff of everyday life. By themselves they are nothing. Yet in the hands of the Master, when consecrated to holy use, it is entirely a different matter. God has promised to receive us at this sacramental meal. Here, our Lord sanctified these elements by his presence to be the spiritual food for our souls. Here, our sins, which may be many, are covered over, forgiven and forgotten. At Holy Communion we come to the Passover of God.

He will pass over all the transgressions of yesterday and those of tomorrow of which we pray, "Forgive us our transgressions." He will pass over all our failures to love and serve him as we should. He will pass over the wrongs we have done to ourselves and to others. Here at this sacrament of Holy Communion, God will bless us and impart to us the consecrated bread and wine of eternal life. Holy Communion is our Passover feast, where all can pass from the things of this world to thoughts of things unseen. Even now the veil has been lifted, and through our faith in Christ Jesus we are enabled to pass into the presence of the Eternal God. And in that future time, in the day of our own appointment when we will have received our call to glory, we will pass from this life to a life of immortality and into the light of our Savior's eternal presence.

THE CONSECRATED BREAD AND WINE

We may view the ceremony at the Last Supper as the pledge extended to us by our Lord in Holy Communion. While the twelve disciples were gathered with their Lord about the table, the low-burning candle was flickering, casting shadows about the room. The disciples were uneasy. This was to be the Savior's last supper with them this side of the cross. Some were troubled with doubt. Some were uncertain, and one had already determined to betray Jesus. The storm of envy and hate was about to break over them, for this was the city that knew not the day of its visitation.

In Remembrance of Me

Would the disciples remember the Savior's words and teachings? After the cross, would they still retain their faith in Christ Jesus? When he had gone to be with the Father, would they have the needed courage and strength to proclaim his Gospel? Already, Jesus was despised and rejected of men. Many who originally came to Jesus no longer followed in the Way. A kingdom of spirit and truth did not appeal to them. They preferred the things that were of Caesar and earthly. But these men about the table were the men that God had given him. And though some were weak, some frail, and others doubting, they had remained with the Lord Jesus.

They had come to Jesus because he had shown them the Father; they had come to him because he had been the way back to God, to grace, and glory. They had become his disciples to learn about God's love and care and about God's Word. They had given their hearts and lives to his cause. Unknown to them, they were about to enter into the fellowship of the Savior's suffering, for it had been given unto them not only to believe in Jesus, but also to suffer for his sake. Having been persuaded of our Lord's Gospel, the disciples were soon to tread in the way that Christ had walked, and all would do so with their own individual cross. In a world that was dying for want of a Savior, they would be persecuted for righteousness' sake.

Our Lord gave them a sign and symbol of his pledge to be with them always, even to the uttermost parts of the earth. This they most surely needed. But the pledge and promise are also for us. Here and now in the midst of our days, Jesus makes himself known to us. He speaks to us the same words, and with the same love, compassion, and sympathetic understanding. Having received the sacrament from the Lord Jesus, St. Paul wrote:

> For I received from the Lord what I also delivered to you, that the Lord Jesus on the night when he was betrayed took bread, and when he had given thanks, he broke it, and said, "This is my body which is [given] for you. Do this in remembrance of me." In the same way also the cup, after supper, saying, "This cup is the new covenant in my blood. Do this, as often as you drink it, in remembrance of me." (1 Cor. 11:23–25 RSV)

"Do this," said our Lord, "in remembrance of me"—in remembrance of my words and gospel; in remembrance of my sacrifice for you. Do this in remembrance of my love and promise to be with you always, even unto the ends of the earth. The disciples had difficulty in comprehending all that Jesus said to them. But they had made a beginning. It was the Spirit that later brought home to them the full significance of all these things. After Christ's death and resurrection, they understood the Savior's spiritual teachings, and they remembered his life, mission, words, and cross.

In the sacredness of this worship hour, amidst the elements of bread and wine, we unite as one to remember our Lord Christ Jesus. We come to pledge to him anew our love, hearts, and loyalty. Let us acknowledge what we do here. We worship him, we share in the Savior's suffering, and we keep alive the memory of his sacrifice and Gospel. In praise and gratitude we acknowledge that Christ Jesus is our Lord, our Savior God, and the Faithful Witness.

The Consecrated Bread and Wine

Holy Communion became the heart and high point of the worship service for the early Church. In the grace of God that was given them, it became the undying flame of their faith. To the church universal, the sacrament has become a means of mystic, sweet communion with Christ. Here, the elements of bread and wine are consecrated by prayer, by the Holy Spirit, and by the presence of Christ. In worship the elements are set apart for holy use. Through prayer and the Holy Spirit, they become infused with the body and blood of our Lord Jesus Christ in a spiritual presence, and become to all of us an impulse of spiritual fortitude. The sacrament becomes the substance of things hoped for, the visible evidence of things unseen. It is a worship service from which the strong sons and daughters of God may go forth in the triumph of their faith. Though hundreds of centuries have passed since this religious ceremony was first instituted, it still retains the power to revive our faith, to encourage faint hearts, and to strengthen feeble knees. We and our church are enabled to resound once again with the strong echoes of the Gospel message.

With the sacrifice of praise and hearts filled with gratitude, we acknowledge the sacred gift that is here set before us. The Eucharist, for all ages, has become the central act of the Church in worship. It comes endowed with the gentle influence of the Spirit, and the Spirit comes to uplift our hearts and empower the life of the

Church. We are reminded that we worship a risen and living Lord. And our Redeemer comes to us in this sacrament exactly as the risen and living Lord, and he comes with unfailing power to transform. The sacrament of Holy Communion is very near the center of all our believing.

In remembering our Lord's sacrifice, here in the eternal testimony of his redemptive work, we confess him as our Savior. We share with him a moment of deep communion, where spirit to spirit speak as we partake of the bread and wine. We become part of that great body, which is the church universal, as we experience again the wonders of his care. Here is revealed the full marvel and mystery of our salvation. It is that moment when we turn again to the Lord Jesus with all our heart, soul, and mind. We acknowledge our reconciliation with him in whom we live, and move, and have our being.

Indeed, as we take these elements of bread and wine into our bodies, we consecrate ourselves to him who has redeemed us through his mercy, and who has brought us nigh through the blood of his cross. And while we bear his sign and seal, we also acknowledge that the nail-scarred hands are forever the marks of his love. This is Holy Communion, the supreme wonder and mystery of our faith, the heart of mystic, sweet communion with Father, Spirit, and Son.

Consecrated and Touched of God

The wonder of Holy Communion is that here in the presence of the consecrated bread and wine we can be touched of God. He comes to us as of old, as he came to those by the Sea of Galilee. In Christ Jesus, God comes assuring us of his steadfastness, of his love and providence. While we worship him, the Lord Jesus comes to touch our hearts and souls. We sense the stirring of his Spirit within us. For, indeed, we have gathered in worship to sense his presence. We have come to the house of God and to the gate of heaven, because our hearts and our souls have cried out for the living God. We come seeking a strengthening hand from the risen

Lord of glory. Here at the Lord's table our hearts have found their quest, and we are filled with the fullness of God.

Even now the Spirit makes intercession for us, and he does so with groanings that cannot be uttered. Here souls will find their heart's desire in the Lord Jesus. At what time we are afraid, we will trust in the Lord. We will trust in him and not be afraid, "For thou Lord only maketh me dwell in safety" (Ps. 4:8). Holy Communion is our Lord's pledge that he will stand by our side, by our heart, and he will whisper to us his words of grace. The consecrated bread and wine are at once a reminder of his pledge, and also a testimony of the hope and faith that live in our hearts. This sacrament is ever a lamp that lights our hearts anew.

We have come at last to this wonderful and marvelous encounter with Christ, where the bread of life is broken to us. And absolutely no one can leave such an encounter with the Lord Jesus empty. We can leave this sanctuary pulsating with spiritual life and a quickened faith. We can leave with the realization that God in Jesus Christ has touched our lives. Thus, in gratitude we consecrate ourselves anew to the cause of our Savior's kingdom. From that obscure Upper Room of long ago, the Gospel evangel has tolled once again, and like the sound of many waters, it has run through the ages of time. Like the feet of those beautiful upon the mountain, this holy sacrament comes to us bringing good news, bringing peace and rest to our souls with the pledge and promise of our faith, touching us with the grace and love of God. Amen.

EMBRACING THE PROMISE

Within its many elements of grace, the sacrament of Holy Communion is also a spiritual encounter, where we may personally embrace and own the promise of our faith. The author of the Epistle to the Hebrews wrote:

> These all died in faith, not having received the promises, but having seen them afar off, and were persuaded of them, and embraced them, and confessed that they were strangers and pilgrims on earth. (Heb. 11:13)

Our Faith Is One of Promise

Our faith is one of promise, and that promise is one of grace, grandeur, and glory. A promise is one's pledge to do something specific, a declaration given to another person. The individual to whom it is made has the right to claim the performance. A promise is also the basis of hope and expectation. Those of us who are married exchanged promises at our wedding. We promised to love and to cherish, in sickness and in health, for better or worse, for richer, for poorer, and we promised till death do us part. With love in our hearts, we embraced those promises made to each other.

The ancient ones of whom the author of the Epistle to the Hebrews wrote were aware of the promises of God. Nevertheless, they did not receive the fulfillment of the promise, nor did they receive the promised One. But by the Spirit of Christ that was in them, they perceived him afar off. In their hearts they were persuaded of Christ, and in faith they embraced him. "The holy men of old" understood the significance of the promised Redeemer. Yet, because of the grandeur and glory of the promised One, they could only conceive of themselves as pilgrims and strangers on Earth.

Of the promise given to us through faith, Simon Peter wrote in his first epistle:

> Of which salvation the prophets inquired and searched diligently, who prophesied of the grace that should come unto you; Searching of what manner of time and Spirit of Christ which was in them did signify; when it testified before hand of the sufferings of Christ, and of the glory that should follow. (1 Pet 1:10, 11)

They prophesied of the grace of our Lord Jesus Christ, of his suffering, and the glory he would obtain because he endured the cross. When the ancient ones saw the wonder of the promise and the absolute glory of the coming Christ, they could only marvel and rejoice in the Almighty, while all the sons of God sang and shouted for joy. We have united in worship at the sacramental table, because the love of God in our hearts and the grace given us evoke a response. We express this promise as we share in the elements of Holy Communion.

United in our Savior's Spirit, we testify to the grace that was given us, to the sufferings of Christ, and to the glory that followed his cross. We remember that the promise was fulfilled in Christ. What more can we do than, as St. Paul, say in our hearts, "Thanks be unto God for his unspeakable gift" (2 Cor. 9:15)?

Embracing the Promise

The ancient ones saw, indeed, from afar, but even so they took possession of the promise, received it into their hearts, and made it their own. To embrace means to cherish and to love. It means to

receive readily and to welcome it and to avail oneself of the promise. This is why we come to the bread of his presence, in order that
we may receive and cherish this sacrament. We come to welcome
it into our hearts and to avail ourselves of the comfort and assurance that it brings. We have come to sense the grace that is given
us at our Lord's table.

We are aware that the duties of our daily life, of our employ-
ment, care of the home, and making the monthly payments have
left us spent. Sometimes it seems as though we have scarcely made
it through another month. And when after a lingering illness, death
has taken a loved one, though our voices utter not a word, our
souls and our hearts sense the need of God. And we need God in
spite of all the fortitude we possess. When death by consumption
had taken one sister, and another sister had now become afflicted
with the disease and was dying, Charlotte Bronte wrote, "Amidst
our family sufferings and death we tried to display fortitude. But
fortitude, I discovered, was not enough. We needed God." And so
do we. Thus it is that we come to the Lord's Supper to sense the
strong hand of God at our side once more. We are bidden to avail
ourselves of the comfort and consolation that Holy Communion
brings when we embrace the promise.

The Grace Given You

> Of which salvations the prophets inquired and searched dili-
> gently; who prophesied of the grace given you. (1 Pet. 1:10)

What is this grace given us and manifested in the elements of
bread and wine? Grace is love and kindness, the kindness of God
toward us in Christ Jesus. It is mercy. It is a state of being favored
where we are exempted from penalty. The grace of our Lord Jesus
Christ is also an attractiveness, a charm, a natural elegance, harmony, and beauty of movement. Grace is also forgiveness, absolution, and reception into the kingdom of heaven. Grace is manifested
in our Savior's promise to be with us always. In the complexities
and struggles of life, in our sufferings, sorrows, and joys, we
can look to the grace of our Lord Jesus Christ. All the above is

included in the grace that has been given us, along with the grace to avail ourselves of its blessings.

When the last enemy, death, has invaded our home, we do not have to sustain the loss of a loved one alone. Our Lord will share our sorrow and grief. His presence can ease the pain of loss. And a sorrow shared is a sorrow lessened. When we are contemplating the resolution of a serious problem, or when the time comes that our youth, strength, and endurance seem to be ebbing away, we can call on our Lord for strength and renewal. We can avail ourselves of the promise. There is not one among the older of us who has not suffered the death of a son, a brother, a daughter, or a parent. We know that grief can afflict our soul at such a time. There is not one among us who has not had a serious problem to resolve, and sometimes they seem to come one after another. Who has never felt his strength and endurance seeming to ebb away? Our souls and spirits become afflicted also. And in the end there is really only One who always strengthens us—Jesus Christ. Thus we come to this sacrament to avail ourselves of our Lord's promise and presence, of his help, love, and grace.

The Glory that Should Follow

> And the Spirit of Christ that was in them testified before hand
> of the sufferings of Christ, and of the glory that should follow.
> (1 Pet. 1:11)

God the Father gave the Holy Spirit to the Church of Jesus Christ. And the Spirit seeks lodging within the believer. This is part of that glory that should follow—our Savior's Spirit dwelling in our hearts. And as we partake of the consecrated bread and wine, we testify to the sufferings of Christ and to the benediction of his cross. We acknowledge that in the keeping of our Savior, our souls and hopes are forever secure. Ours is a mystical faith, and yet it is very real and practical. It is a constant and present help for all our needs. This is another aspect of the grace and glory that was given us.

The sharing of the bread and wine, as is our Savior's kingdom, is open to all who seek the Lord God. It is open to all that know or would know Christ as Savior and Lord. For the Savior's coming was an invitation to us. This is the Lord's table. He extended an invitation to all that hunger and thirst, to all the heavy-laden, and to all who seek rest for their souls. There is nobility and grace for grace in the length and breadth of our Lord's invitation. There is no condition precedent. One simply has to come and confess his need of Christ and the end is grace and glory. Therefore, with gratitude we shall embrace the promise. We will keep warm and alive the love and Spirit of Christ that is within us. Amen.

5

BREAD OF HEAVEN

In his *Apology*, Justin Martyr wrote to Antonius Pius, the emperor, and to Marcus Aurelius, who would soon be emperor, about the concept and practice of the early Church, concerning Holy Communion.

Then to the president of the brethren are brought bread and a cup of wine mixed with water. He takes them and offers praise and glory to the Father of all, in the name of the Son, and of the Holy Spirit; and he gives thanks, that at length we are counted worthy to receive these things at his hands. And when he has concluded the prayers and thanksgiving, the whole people present, assent, saying, "Amen." The men called deacons give to each of those present a portion of the bread and wine mixed with water, over which thanksgiving was pronounced.

This food is called among us, the Eucharist. For not as common bread and as common drink do we receive them; but even as Jesus Christ our Savior, being made flesh by the word of God, took on flesh and blood for our salvation, so likewise we are taught that the food which is blessed by the prayer of his word, and from the transmutation therefrom, our blood and flesh are nourished. And we believe that this is the flesh and blood of

Jesus who was made flesh. For Jesus took bread, and when he had given thanks said: This do in remembrance of me; this is my body; and after the same manner he took the cup, and gave thanks and said: This is my blood, and gave it to his disciples alone. (*First Apology*, Justin Martyr, AntiNecian Fathers, Vol I)

Justin Martyr described the order of worship of the early Church during the celebration of Holy Communion. Bread and wine mixed with water were brought before the worship leader. Then he offered praise and glory to God in prayer, in the name of the Son and in the name of the Holy Spirit. He gave thanks, expressing gratitude to God. He expressed gratitude that Christ had made the congregation worthy to receive the bread and wine.

The elements of communion were not looked upon as common bread and common drink. The early Church believed that the elements blessed by prayer and the word were transmuted (changed) into another nature and substance. Justin Martyr likened the transmutation of the elements to the miracle of the incarnation, in which Jesus took on flesh and blood for our salvation. The early Church believed that the bread and wine of Holy Communion became the flesh and blood of Jesus. The elements transmuted by prayer and the word nourished their flesh and blood.

We can conceive Holy Communion as the Bread of Heaven. And as did our Savior, we may make a mystical and spiritual application of the bread and wine. To the multitude of long ago, our Lord said, "Do not labor for the food which perishes, but for the food which endures to eternal life, which the Son of man will give you: for on him has God the Father set his seal" (John 6:27).

Bread of Heaven

"But Master," they said, "we really want to do the works of God. What must we do to do the works of God?" Jesus answered, "This is the work of God, that you believe on him whom he has sent."

"To believe in you? This is the work of God? But what signs, what miracles do you perform that we may see and believe in you?

Our fathers ate manna in the wilderness, as it is written; He gave them bread from heaven to eat." "Yes," said Jesus, "my Father gave the true bread from heaven; and the bread of God is that which comes down from heaven and gives life to the world." "Lord," the multitude replied, "give us always this bread." Jesus said:

> I am the bread of life: he that cometh to me shall never hunger; and he that believeth on me shall never thirst. . . . All that the Father giveth me shall come to me: and he that cometh to me I will in no wise cast out. (John 6:35–37)

> But they murmured at him because he said I am the bread which came down from heaven. "Do not murmur," Jesus answered. "No one can come to me unless the Father who sent me draw him." (John 6:43–44)

The words of our Lord are quite plain:

> I am the living bread which came down from heaven: if any one eats of this bread, he will live for ever; and the bread that I will give is my flesh, which I will give for the life of the world. (John 6:51)

Jesus had made a mystical and spiritual application of his body and blood. But the mystical and spiritual use of the body and blood of our Lord Jesus had left the multitude of long ago stupefied. They were too dull of spirit to take it in. They were earthbound. Nevertheless, the mystical and spiritual application of the body and blood of Christ to us is the application of himself to our redemption. Justin Martyr made this application when he said that the bread and wine nourish our souls. And as our Lord Jesus continued with the spiritual application, he said, "He who eats of my flesh and drinks of my blood, abides in me; and I in him" (John 6:56).

We must take the bread and wine into our own bodies, because in so doing we share in the spiritual benefit of our Lord's sacrifice. The teaching is this: that in coming to our Lord's table, we are partakers of his sacrifice; we are taken to the cross with him; we are taken to that place where an end was made of all our sins. As we worship, we feel and know that in this sacrament Christ our Lord has come to us again. He comes to us as the Bread of Heaven with an aura of truth and grace.

Our Spiritual Want Is Met

In the early Church, the communion service was looked upon as a sacrament in which the bread and wine were consecrated, distributed to the congregation, and consumed in commemoration of the passion and death of Christ. In consuming the bread and wine, the people were nourished. "To nourish" means to furnish with food or other material to sustain life. Hence, in Holy Communion, the early Church believed that they were fed with the heavenly manna, which sustained and strengthened their spiritual life. For the believer, Holy Communion, generally, is a religious ceremony subsequent to salvation and church membership. But as a means of grace, it is open to all that would come.

> Ho, every one that thirsteth, come ye to the waters, and he that hath no money; come ye, buy, and eat; yea, come, buy wine and milk without money and without price. Wherefore do ye spend money for that which is not bread? and your labor for that which satisfieth not? (Is. 55:1–2)

As it does in no other service, the Church, in the ceremony of Holy Communion, satisfies the longing, the deep need, and the spiritual yearning of our souls. Our souls have cried out, "Abba, Father" and here that cry has been met.

At the celebration of the Eucharist, the Spirit waits for us to respond to the words of the hymn, "Spirit of the living God, fall afresh on me. Fill me, feed me, till I want no more." In communion with our God, our Savior, and the Holy Spirit, here is offered to us once again the Bread of Heaven. But how do we receive it? While the elements are blessed in prayer and thanksgiving, we cleanse the thoughts of our minds and we assent to the prayers of thanksgiving and praise. We turn our thoughts to God and our mind is stayed on him. We acknowledge the love of our Savior who gave himself for us and who is coming to us again in the elements of bread and wine. We wait in anticipation of his touch as the elements come to us.

In Christ the Promise Is Secure

Simple words these and yet profound and full of meaning: "All that the Father gives me will come to me; and him who comes to me I will never cast out." The Lord Jesus said this in conjunction with his words about the Bread of Heaven. Why did he say this? To give us a sense of security about our faith in him and the efficacy of his atonement which the sacrament represents. To be secure means free from exposure to danger. It means dependable, not liable to fail. It also means free from care and emotionally secure. In the sacrament of Holy Communion, as we think about our Lord's words, the elements of bread and wine speak to us about the certainty given to us by Christ's words. Our Savior's promise and God's Word are surely dependable and not liable to fail, and we can trust our all on that.

While we cannot be free from all care that life may bring upon us, we can be emotionally secure in our relationship with Christ our Lord. He knows our hearts, our thoughts, and our desires. And to our Master, each stands or falls. Having taken into our bodies the bread and wine, we can rest in quiet security. Our soul is fed, the mind is at ease, and the heart is at rest. Out of passion and pain comes peace again as we are nourished by the Bread of Heaven.

6

A Symbol in Faith

Speaking from his view and knowledge of the past, Dr. Carl Jung proved to be a seer. He compared the past influence of Christian symbols to that of their present place in the religious life of an individual. He also expressed his opinion of what force, if any, Christian symbols may have on an individual in the future. Over four decades ago he wrote in *The Atlantic Monthly*:

> As at the beginning of the Christian Aeon, so again today we are faced with the problem of the moral backwardness which has not kept pace with our scientific, technical, and social development. So much is at stake, and so much depends on the inner constitution of man. Does he know that he is on the point of losing the life-preserving symbols of the inner man which Christianity has treasured up for him?

We are losing the meaning, spiritual impact, and power that the symbols of our faith once had on the inner man.

The Symbolic Meaning

We who serve the Church understand that the images and symbols of our faith that once had a vital effect on the soul and heart of man seem to have lost their power over him. Modern man appears lost and confused as to their purpose and meaning. Symbols move us inwardly, because they awaken images of spiritual things. They stir the memory of past religious experience. They also bring to mind various tenets of our faith and keep alive the hope they represent. They represent the spiritual realities of our faith. And quite obviously, when the faith that gives meaning and courage to human life becomes diminished, confusion and paralysis of spirit will be the result. We must ask ourselves, "Have the symbolic and spiritual meaning of our faith grown dim and distant from us, or is it our neglect and obscurity of inner vision that have caused them to lose their significance?"

Generally, the cause for the diminished influence of our Christian symbols is neglect and obscurity of inner vision. We may have forgotten about our symbols or have been too busy with other things to give them much mind. And could we have neglected them because we think that they are too liturgical or because we think that they are incidents of another Christian communion? Christian symbols belong to the church universal. They remind us all of what we believe. More likely, it is obscurity of inner vision that has caused our symbols to lose their impact on us. By inner, I mean that which is related to the spiritual, inner life. Vision is the power to sense things. And by inner vision, I mean the power of sensing our symbols' religious meaning for us. When we permit our faith to lie dormant, unused, or grow weak, spiritual vision is obscured. When this occurs, our symbols do not nourish our souls as they should. It is not without reason then that we ask, "Are the symbols of our faith real and present to us as they were in the beginning of the Christian Aeon?"

Is it possible that the meaning of our Christian symbols has grown weak because we have passed over lightly their spiritual significance? Symbols such as the cup and bread of Holy Communion, the lighting of the candles at the beginning of the worship service, baptism, and our Savior's up-lifted cross are rich and full of spiritual meaning. They were meant to affect the inner man. They speak silently of higher things, of the hope and aspirations of the soul. They speak of God's love and long suffering with us, of the grace of our Lord Jesus Christ, and of the urging of the Holy Spirit. They are symbols of God's grace, real and present with us. They evoke our faith, touch our hearts, and awaken our soul with the spirit and power of an endless life.

The dove, the chalice, the bread and wine, the water and the blood, Spirit and Truth, the candles and the burning of incense, the brazen serpent in the wilderness, and the up-lifted cross are the substance of things hoped for and received, the evidence of things not seen. And yet, it is only our perception, our faith, and the work of the Holy Spirit that makes our Christian symbols real and vital. They are as real and full of spiritual meaning as the Savior who tasted death on the cross because he loved us. We need only to open up our lives and hearts to these symbols once again, and they will become vital and alive to our souls.

Holy Communion, a Symbol of Love and Sacrifice

Holy Communion is a symbol and image of our Lord's love and sacrifice for us, while it reminds us also that the promises of our faith "are yea and Amen" in Christ Jesus. From age to age and from month to month, this sacred ceremony has been repeated times without number, and more likely than not repeated word for word. Holy Communion never loses its appeal to our souls as long as its meaning and purpose are clear, as long as it holds a deep spiritual significance for us. Holy Communion appeals by its power to attract, by its ability to stimulate the mind and emotions. In the end, the secret of its appeal lies in its ability to touch the human heart.

The meaning of the sacrament is that which it is intended to be, the purpose for which our Lord instituted the sacrament—to awaken the memory of his love, sacrifice, and promise. The purpose for which it exists is to support and sustain the spiritual life of the communicant. And its deep spiritual significance is a matter of consequence to the believer. Should one not hold the sacrament in high esteem or fail to attend its celebration, he suffers loss in the strength of his inner life. He will be as one who does not seek oil for his lamp and who simply sits back and watches the flame slowly die out. But let him come to the wells of grace. Let the appeal of the sacrament stimulate his mind with the memory of our Lord's love and sacrifice and the sacrament cannot fail to move his heart.

This sacrament has never failed to appeal to all that seek God. It has never failed to do so partly because of its mystery and partly because of its spiritual influence. Each of us can enter into that meaning because part of that meaning is within each of us. We have been created with the potential of becoming what God has intended us to be. Stirring in the deepest recesses of our souls there is an invisible helper, the Holy Spirit, which is the creative and spiritual power imaged in the Lord's Supper. The bread when broken and the wine when served are the visible evidence of what occurred on the cross. According to the will of our heavenly Father, the Lord Jesus, on the cross, gave his life as an offering for the world's confusion, darkness, and sins. While the ceremony recalls the cross, it is symbolic of hope, of inner nourishment, and of the creative spirit of our religion. That spiritual grace reaches out to us from the night when Holy Communion was first instituted by our Lord. And like the Spirit of the living God, the symbolic impact of this sacrament reaches for us across the centuries of time. The inward grace of our faith has lost none of its power to hold the heart and soul of man. If the meaning of our Christian symbols has become dim, it is because we have not permitted the faith they represent to touch our hearts and to penetrate deeply into the inner man.

Part of the problem may lie in the fact that we do not think of asking how the inner man feels about the things we do in the outside world. But if we do have the courage to inquire, we would receive the answer from a still small voice imaged in the Spirit of our Redeemer. We cannot neglect our spiritual life and expect to be free from all mental and emotional disturbance. So much depends on the human soul and its disposition. Without the soul, and the creative, spiritual aspect it gives to life, the world would be more like a jungle than like a human society. In the many decisions one must make in the course of life, he cannot decide properly if he is spiritually undernourished. Reminding himself of the meaning of our Christian symbols and of the meaning of Holy Communion here at the Lord's table, the believer is nourished by more than a mere earthly source of power.

We hunger for many things: for righteousness, for beauty, for security, and love. God has put these hungers in us to bring us to himself and to bring us to that life in Christ Jesus, by which all our hungers are satisfied. And it is his love that can make our drooping spirits soar. Here at the sacrament, if we are attentive to its meaning, the hunger for a richer spiritual life is met. This too is one of the symbolic meanings and mysteries of Holy Communion. And as we worship, the Spirit touches our inner man and confirms our unspoken prayers. Here, even the weak and the not so worthy can experience the King in all his glory and move a little closer to his likeness.

We Respond to the Silent, Symbolic Appeal

In our souls we experience anew the reality of our spiritual union with Christ Jesus. Our hearts respond to the silent appeal of these symbols of our faith: the bread and wine. Our worship confirms that Holy Communion has the spiritual grace to nourish our souls. We become aware of its spiritual impact under the influence of the Spirit. We share in a vital religious experience, which is the heart of our faith, bringing us into immediate communion with our Lord. In our souls and thoughts, our spiritual expectations are awakened to an acute awareness. We worship in awed silence as we contemplate the thought Jesus loved us enough to give his life for us.

We also contemplate the thought that as often as we eat this bread and drink this cup we proclaim the Lord's death until he comes. We may not know how or in what manner our heavenly Father will cause the kingdoms of the world to be transformed into the kingdoms of our Lord, or even if the world appreciates our Lord's present kingdom of peace and righteousness. For those who believe in the Second Advent of our Lord, the future holds no fear. It holds the expectation of wonder and grace. It will be a time when all the mysteries of life shall be ultimately resolved. Yet we are persuaded that having placed our faith in Christ Jesus, we shall see the consummation of all our hopes, in so far as they rest in him. This is what the believer should do always: rest his hope in Christ Jesus.

Thinking on the meaning of our Christian symbols, on the spiritual power they bring to our inner man and resting our hope in Christ, we can leave the sacrament table with souls that rest in peace. We can leave with the courage to do the will of God in the world, insofar as he has made us able. Believing in Holy Communion as a strong and vital symbolic ceremony of spiritual realities present with us and as giving nourishment to our inner man, we will have been fortified with the grace of God. As we commemorate once again his sacrifice on the cross, our hearts and our minds tell us that his kingdom comes and that his kingdom is within.

7

IN REMEMBRANCE OF ME

In Arlington National Cemetery there is a perpetual flame at the grave of President John F. Kennedy. The flame is a memorial of this particular president. Neither his family nor the nation desired that his memory die out. It was hoped that this flame would serve to keep alive the ideals and dreams that he had for the nation. That flame was lit over a quarter of a century ago.

What do we remember about President Kennedy? Perhaps little, perhaps much. We who are older recall some things about him. We remember that his tragic death came as a shock to the entire nation. We remember that he was a young president who seemed to flood the Capitol with youth. We recall what he looked like, his short hair, broad smile, and happy face. We may remember part of his inaugural address, but beyond this our memory grows dim. His image fades away, and this was only a little over a quarter century ago.

Our Lord Jesus said, "Do this in remembrance of me" (1 Cor. 11:24). A memory is a strange and fascinating thing. Sometimes it is sharp and clear, and at other times it is dim and hazy. We can't seem to put all the details together. The more we try, the more the memory seems to recede.

The Fading of a Memory

With the passage of time a memory becomes obscure. We have difficulty in keeping the image of our dearest memories clear. Charles Dickens, looking back on some of the works of his early youth, is reported to have remarked, "What a genius I was when I wrote that." He meant that in the intervening years, he had lost the dreams, visions, and ideals of his younger days. The memory of what he had once set out to do still troubled him. It lay in the deep recesses of his mind obscured by time and neglect. Once it was sharp and clear, flooding his consciousness, but no longer. He failed to keep it alive and it faded away.

We might ask ourselves, "What do we keep in remembrance?" Have we lost all the images of the past? Have the things of yesterday become forgotten and forsaken dreams? Have we allowed the passage of time or the dull chores of life to lay a blanket over our memory? Does the flame still burn there? Do we still retain the ideals of love, hope, and faith in our hearts? Do we still remember the grace and love of our Lord Jesus Christ and all that it means to us? We acknowledge that there are difficulties. Sometimes we are unable to remember because our memory is not very good. At other times we can't remember because our minds won't let us. Some people remember only the worst things, while others remember only the good things. And there are those individuals who do not wish to remember at all.

There are still other persons whose memories of the past have made them bitter. They only remember misfortune, the broken trust, a misplaced confidence, a grave disappointment, and broken faith. They perceive today and tomorrow as only a repetition of the past. And yet the sad thing is that keeping such memories of the past alive affects their emotions and attitude toward life. Everything seems to turn sour for them. What can they do to consciously put behind them the memory of things they cannot forget? They can flood the mind with new rays of light. They can work to consciously memorize passages from the Scriptures that are uplifting. They can work to memorize some of the helpful Psalms, such as the fourth, eighth, eleventh, sixteenth, and twenty-sixth Psalms.

Actually, in the foreground of consciousness, the mind can hold only so much. The good thoughts, the inspirational passages, will push out of their mind the things they would like to forget. They can lean on the memory of the Psalms. It is good to do so, because one cannot live under the weight of past difficulties. Even the strong will eventually break under such a load. Memorizing uplifting passages of the Scriptures will lead them to discover that "God has not given us the spirit of fear; but of power, and of love, and of a sound mind" (2 Tim. 1:7).

While there is the cover of difficulties that may obscure the memory, there is also the enhanced clearness of pleasant memories. Memories can be rewarding, acting as the background of deep and rich experiences. We can draw strength from them, hope from them, and peace from them. They can engender the impulses that feed a wholesome life. A good memory can dwell in our hearts and make us glad that we are alive. The words of St. Paul are helpful, "retain the good." It can prove to be a storehouse for tomorrow.

When my father died, I was twenty-five years old, and I remember everything about him that was good. He was a man, so he had his faults. But what a man he was. I remember the way he walked, the way he talked, and how he always came straight to the heart of a matter with one clear stroke. I can say that I learned about fatherhood from him. Through the grace of our Lord Christ Jesus, I managed to retain the good about him in my memory. A memory of our loved ones can be one of the better treasures of our lives. It can fill our hearts with love, hope, and faith, and we must not let it fade away.

The Reality of Our Savior's Memory

Jesus said, "Do this in remembrance of me." He told us to remember, to search back in our hearts and thoughts to that time of high spiritual experience. Why did he tell us to remember? Because our Lord knew that without some tie to the past, the future is meaningless. The ancient prophets were constantly telling the people to remember their tie with the past, how God had delivered them from bondage in Egypt, how he had brought them to a goodly land, flowing with milk and honey. The prophets also reminded the people how they had promised to love and serve God with all their hearts, all their souls, and all their minds. Whenever they forgot their tie with the past, they lost their perspective and things went wrong. But as long as they remembered their relationship with God, things went right for them.

What do we remember about Jesus of Nazareth? We are not sure of how he looked. We really do not know whether his hair was long or short. Nor do we actually know the color of his eyes. Most of the paintings of Jesus, which originate in the mind of the painter, differ one from another. And none of us can say which one of the paintings is closer to the truth. What, then, are we to remember about our Lord and Savior? What is it that we should keep in remembrance? And what is there about him that can keep our love, faith, and hope alive?

We are to remember who he was, what he said, and what he did. We are to remember his love and sacrifice and his Gospel of grace. We are to remember that if we have known him, then we have known the Father, also. In the sacrament of Holy Communion, we are to remember that his body was given because he loved us and that his blood was shed for many for the remission of sins. This holy sacrament, wherein we partake of the consecrated bread and wine, serves to keep that memory sharp and clear. As often as we do this in remembrance of our Lord, it will serve to keep our memory of Jesus very much alive. It will keep our Lord's memory from fading away.

Now our Lord said many things, but on this occasion, I want to leave only one of his sayings with you: "Peace I leave with you, my peace I give unto you . . . Let not your heart be troubled, neither let it be afraid" (John 14:27). Who has never had a troubled heart? Who has never been afraid at one time or another? Who has never suffered a loss or undergone misfortune? And who has never felt sorrow or grief? Again, at one time or another, we all have. As we remember our Lord's grace and love for us, his absolution and reception, we can come to this sacrament with troubled hearts. We remember that here the troubled in heart will find rest and peace for their souls.

We are also aware that these elements of bread and wine are simple things and that in themselves they can preserve no memory. But in the hands of the Master all is changed and everything becomes new. He gives these elements spiritual meaning, and his grace and Spirit work a miracle of transformation. They become incidents in our memory of inward spiritual grace. The bread and wine bring into focus that our Lord's body was given and his blood was shed because Jesus loved us. These consecrated elements have become the food of our souls and the living impulse of our spirits. The memory of holy things lives in us once again, and in spite of ourselves we think back on God's blessings and on his promises for the future.

What are your memories? The good ones and the bitter ones? The ones that haunt you, and the ones that bless you. What are the memories that have grown dim and the ones that are sharp and clear? Which are the ones that cause you pain and the ones that fill your days with joy and strength?

We come once again to the sacramental table. And we are bidden to come just as we are, with all of our memories, anxieties, doubts, and fears. Though we may come with all these shades of memory to the sacramental table, we come with faith and hope. We come with God's Word deep in our hearts. We will ask once again that our Lord cleanse the memories of our mind, that he purge out the bitter ones, the painful ones, and the haunting ones. We will dwell on the good things that we have gleaned from God's Word, which are the words of life and beauty. God has promised to receive us on his holy ground. This body was given for us and this blood was shed for many for the remission of sins. Our Savior is present with us to bring us the memory of his love and grace and the memory of our heavenly Father's providence.

Our Savior will take our memories and, while expunging the bad ones, he can retain for us the good, making them sharp and clear once more. As we make ready to receive this holy sacrament, let us do so in remembrance of him. Let us ask that, as he cleanses our thoughts, that he also illumine our minds and quicken our hearts. As we hold these spiritual tokens in our hands, in heartfelt thanks to Christ our Lord, let us apply to our souls the bread of life.

Prayer

Almighty God, thou art the light and salvation of all thy people, and thou art the strength of our life. All our times are in thy hands, and for this shall every one that is godly pray unto thee in a time when thou mayest be found. For thou wilt hear from heaven and in thy mercy answer us, O God of our salvation.

Almighty Spirit, let not thy people be forgotten like those who are forgotten time out of mind, and neither let the memory of past blessings die out altogether in us. Let us hold thy goodness in remembrance. Remove from us the slowness of heart, the dullness of memory, and the sins that obscure that we may see thee and worship thee as thou art.

Almighty Savior, let thy presence be with us at this hour for we have gathered at thy communion table. Let the body that was broken and the blood that was shed be unto us the true bread of life. And grant, eternal Savior, that what we have received with our mouths, we may keep in believing hearts. And may this holy sacrament ever lead us unto life everlasting. Amen.

8

Bread and Wine and an Endless Priesthood

In the old dispensation, God at many times and in different manners revealed the promise of the coming Redeemer. This was done to give his people hope and to make known his provision for them. The Lord God has revealed his purpose of mercy in Scriptures, history, and in the incidents of human lives. He did so on one occasion in the life of Abraham.

> Melchizedek king of Salem brought forth bread and wine: and he was the priest of the most high God. And he blessed him, and said, Blessed be Abram of the most high God, possessor of heaven and earth. (Gen. 14:18–19)

> The Lord said unto my Lord, Sit thou on my right hand, until I make thine enemies thy footstool . . . in the beauty of holiness from the womb of the morning: thou hast the dew of thy youth. The Lord hath sworn, and shall not repent, Thou art a priest, forever, after the order of Melchizedek. (Ps. 110:1–4)

In this encounter, the king of Salem brought forth bread and wine as an offering and as refreshment for Abraham. Involved in this ceremony was the concept of a priesthood created after the power of an endless life.

The Incident

The kings of the north plundered Sodom and Gomorrah, and they carried away Lot, Abraham's nephew, along with many others. News of this raid reached Abraham. He armed his own band, was joined by three local chieftains, Ener, Eschol, and Mamre, and went in pursuit of the kings of the north. In the dead of night they fell upon the raiders, inflicted a great slaughter upon them and regained the spoils. All was brought back, including Lot and the captives. Then, entirely unexpected, the king of Salem came to bless Abraham and to refresh him with bread and wine. This was the priest-king Melchizedek, who is identified as the priest of the most high God. Abraham bowed before him to receive the blessing and gave Melchizedek a tenth of all the spoils.

Bread and wine, the elements of Holy Communion, were brought to Abraham by this priest-king whose coming was like a sudden ray of light. He appeared suddenly, unexpectedly, mysteriously, and then, just as quickly, he was gone. In this sudden brief appearance of the priest-king, the Church has always seen a brief flash of light of ancient revelation. Like a shooting star streaking across the heavens, there appears a forerunner of Christ. He was a shadow and a type pointing and looking forward to the coming of the Promised One. There was also a shadow of the sacramental table with the elements of bread and wine. These elements could only speak silently of our Lord's sacrifice, of the cross, and the atonement of Jesus Christ.

Righteousness and Peace

Although Genesis is silent about his sudden appearance and disappearance, Hebrews and the Psalms give us information on the spiritual significance of the priest-king, Melchizedek. His name means "king of righteousness" and his government is identified as that of the prince of peace. And the bread and wine brought as an offering by him are elements symbolizing the kingdom of righteousness and peace. This realm points to the kingdom where truth and spirit reign and where the weary may find rest for their souls and peace for their hearts.

In the Epistle to the Hebrews, we are informed that Melchizedek, king of Salem, who blessed Abraham, was the priest of the most high God. The righteousness spoken of is the righteousness that is given by God's grace. It points to the righteousness bestowed by faith upon believers. It comes as a gift of God's love. The blessing bestowed upon Abraham by the priest-king Melchizedek was of peace and righteousness. And, as to the promise of his own life, Abraham believed the Lord God, and his faith was accounted unto him for righteousness. So it is with us today. Our Lord's kingdom, where righteousness dwells, means the righteousness of Jesus Christ, which we obtain by faith in him. Like Melchizedek, Christ is a king of righteousness and peace. And thus, when consecrated to holy use, the elements of bread and wine symbolize the essential concepts of our Savior's kingdom, which are righteousness and peace: "For the Lord has sworn and will not repent: thou art a priest forever after the order of Melchizedek."

The Unique Order of His Priesthood

When this brief revelation of light invaded the history of the kingdom, it revealed that the priesthood of Christ was of a high and unique order. Melchizedek was not a priest after the order of Aaron, nor Abraham, but of a distinct and unique calling. As to the forerunner's lineage, he appeared without father, without mother; having neither beginning of days, nor end of life. "But made like unto the Son of God; and abideth a priest continually," forever, after the power of an endless life.

> And it is yet far more evident; for that after the similitude of Melchizedek there ariseth another priest. Who is made after the power of an endless life. (Heb 7:15–16)

The concept is one of an endless priesthood. The priests of the Aaronic order ended their days on Earth and all were taken by death. But our Lord lives forever to carry on his ministry of intercession and to reign over his kingdom as God's exalted Son. Though the bread is broken and consumed together with the wine, they are symbols of our Lord's endless ministry of intercession. The priest is one who makes absolution and intercession for his people. His ministry is an intercession of love, grace, and unbounded forgiveness. His ministry also brings the people to a state of righteousness and peace and joy in the Holy Spirit. Our Lord's interceding Spirit touches the heart and soul of those who acknowledge him as Lord. In partaking of the bread and wine at Holy Communion, we are reminded that we have received absolution.

While Melchizedek was identified as the king of peace and righteousness, our Savior is all that and more. He is in our hearts through his Spirit and at the right hand of God exalted. He makes intercession above and covers us over with the righteousness of his grace and gives us the confirmation of the Holy Spirit. The transition was from an Aaronic service, primarily of outward conformity, to our Lord's kingdom, where the worship is essentially inward and spiritual. However great and glorious may have been the priestly order of Melchizedek, he was no more than a limited figure and type of Christ our Lord.

The bread and wine are symbols of our Lord's endless priesthood, of absolution, and of the law written in our hearts. In giving the Holy Spirit to our Savior's Church, the Lord God promised: "I will put my laws in their inward parts, and write them in their hearts" (Jer. 31:33) The law written into our hearts is the law of the Spirit, and the Spirit comes as an abiding and sanctifying presence. Our Savior's grace has a moral effect on our thoughts, feelings, and actions. The moral effect of the Holy Spirit is direct, primary, and permanent. When the Holy Spirit dwells and works in a human life, the outcome leads to spiritual gifts and understanding.

We thank God for the forerunners like Melchizedek, who first brought to light the elements of bread and wine. We thank God for the prophets and "the holy men of old." And yet they may have been like the voice of God speaking of his providence in times past, telling us of good things to come.

When we come to the consecrated elements of bread and wine, we need not worry if at times we are unable to formulate the proper words of prayer. The Holy Spirit will do it for us. Nor should we hesitate to bring our burdens and heartaches to the Lord. The Savior is here at the table of intercession, and the Comforter has come alongside to help. Our Lord is gracious. He understands the infirmities of our flesh and he knows how to deal with the slow of heart. We need only think of the concept of prayer. The words can be short, simple, and direct. The paraclete who has come alongside to help is our advocate with the Father, and in Holy Communion, he has come to apply to our hearts the grace of our Lord Jesus Christ. Amen.

9

GATHER UP THE FRAGMENTS

One day when the Master had concluded his work, he instructed the disciples, saying, "Gather up the fragments that remain, that nothing be lost" (John 6:12). In the celebration of Holy Communion we express our unity in Christ. We have one faith, one God, and one Lord. We are one in Christ the world over.

We know from the Gospel narrative that there were times when Jesus saw the people as broken and fragmented. They gave the impression of sheep scattered about and without a shepherd. Many were indifferent to our Lord's Gospel and the things he said about God and life. Others, because of poverty or neglect of spiritual things, appeared as broken bits of humanity. They lacked that wholesomeness of life conducive to spiritual and moral well being.

What is a fragment? It is a small part broken off. It is broken off from a whole. Take a beautiful vase and smash it onto the floor. What do you have? Fragments. What good is a fragment? Not much. Most of us would simply sweep up the fragments and dump them in a trash can. Who really wishes to be bothered by fragments, anyway? Nevertheless, the Lord Jesus said, "Gather up the fragments . . . that nothing be lost." Jesus had it in mind to save the fragments, the broken and unfulfilled bits of humanity of this world.

But a vase, a piece of bread, these are not the only things that can be broken. A human life can be broken just as surely as a potter takes his vessels and smashes them against a stone. What does it mean to be broken or fragmented? It means to be separated from that which makes and keeps us whole. As we apply it to our moral and spiritual well being, it means to be separated from God, from the healing touch of his Spirit, and from the grace of our Lord Jesus Christ. It means to go our own indifferent way and not take God or the leading of the Spirit into our plans. To find oneself estranged from the grace that can keep us whole and wholesome can occur to any human being. The saddest thing to see is a life that is only a detached piece of a once beautiful self. It is no great sin to outlive our generation or to be like the last leaf on a tree. But for one to allow the light of hope and purpose to be put out or to lose the spirit of faith and love even for a single day is a tragic thing. Without faith, hope, and love, we can never be a completely whole person.

There are situations encountered that make life seem harsh and on occasion more like a grindstone. But whether these incidents grind a person down or build endurance in his character depends on the love and strength of the Spirit that resides within him. But there is assuredly the possibility that any life, be it great or small, may be broken long before it is committed to the ground.

Friendships can also disintegrate. As with any other possession or treasure, we tend to take advantage of friendships. We neglect them, or use them, or even smash them. Elizabeth Barrett Browning once asked Charles Kingsley what was the secret of his kind and understanding life. He is said to have replied: "I had a friend." And so do we. Our Savior said, "No longer do I call you servants, but friends" (John 15:15 RSV). A friend had helped to make Charles Kingsley's life beautiful and gave him understanding. We have a Savior-Friend, and his grace can make our life beautiful, and understanding also. We can accumulate a good treasure in friendships, and good friends enrich human life.

Love can be strong, sensitive, and enduring. Still, we continually place it under stress. We place it under stress until it snaps and becomes shattered beyond recognition. In her poem, "The Sleep," Elizabeth Barrett Browning wrote:

> What do we give our beloved?
> A little faith all undisproved,
> A little dust to overweep,
> And bitter memories to make,
> The whole earth blasted for our sake:
> God giveth his beloved sleep.
>
> "Sleep soft," beloved! we sometimes say,
> We who have no tune to charm away
> Sad dreams that through the eyelids creep:
> O earth, so full of dreary noises!
> O men, with wailing in your voices!
> O deviled gold, the wailers heap!
> O strife, o curse, that o'er it fall!
> God strike a silence through you all,
> And giveth his beloved sleep.

There are times when having viewed the broken fragments of humanity strewn about that we can only pray that God would, indeed, strike a silence through it all. When we see the broken lives, shattered friendships, and loves lost, we pray that God forgive us for rushing through life, scattering broken fragments in every direction. Through his grace, in communion with our Lord at this hour, we remind ourselves that he loves us with a love that never fails. In silently confessing our sins of neglect, the bread and wine assure us of our Savior's compassion—his love covers a multitude of sins.

Why the Fragments?

We are interested in the reason why lives become fragmented. We wonder whether a cross can cause fragmentation. In the discharge of his mission, the Lord Jesus endured the agony of his cross. He instructed those who chose to follow him to first take up their cross. In the last analysis, life cannot be entirely separated from a cross. But we are convinced that crosses do not break lives. Nor do hardships shatter friendships. And love is not dashed into pieces because of suffering. These painful incidents in our lives may be more like the refiner's fire, burning away the slag. We must look elsewhere for the cause of fragmentation.

Quite possibly the cause of fragmentation may be that we have lost the vision and influence of God's glory, grace, and grandeur. Vision is the ability to look ahead or to see things in a wider perspective. Influence is the effect such a vision or wider perspective has on us, on our inner life. God's glory is the splendor of his majesty mirrored in creation. His grace is his kindly disposition toward them that turn to him. And God's grandeur is the awesome greatness of his person and power. Nothing is too difficult for him, and with God all things are possible. That we have such a God who cares for us and is mindful of us can influence the integrity and spiritual strength of our lives. But if we have lost our vision of his grace and grandeur, God's spiritual influence in our lives is diminished and our lives can begin to disintegrate.

Having lost the vision of God's glory, grace, and grandeur, we will forget about the strength and power of that great Rock under whom we have come to trust. As we view God, we also view the Son. Our relationship with Christ is paramount to our spiritual life. And the strength of this relationship depends on the strength and power we attribute to our Lord. He gives meaning and purpose to our lives in relation to God, in relation to each other, and in relation to this world and the next. And to neglect the strength of our relationship with Christ can cause us to lose the concept of purpose and meaning for our lives. Joseph Wood Crutch, a man who seemed devoid of all faith, wrote: "There is no reason to suppose that a man's life has any more meaning than that of the humblest, crawling insect." We comprehend his meaning clearly: if life does not matter, what then is there to hold it together? There is nothing to keep it from falling apart.

How Does Fragmentation Occur?

How does fragmentation occur? What are the consequences? More meaning than an insect? The words of Jesus certainly speak to this query: "Fear not little flock, for our Father watches over the sparrow; and you are worth more than many sparrows." Simple words these and not too difficult to understand. But we lose their significance in the roar of the football arena. We forget their meaning in the friendly chatter of a bridge game. And we overlook them in the unswerving pursuit of our own endeavor. There are other phrases spoken by our Lord that aid us in finding meaning and purpose to life. "Seek ye first the kingdom of God and his righteousness . . . I am the resurrection and the life . . . Greater love hath no man than this, that a man lay down his life for a friend."

Life may well fall apart because one has forgotten simple admonitions. One may let caution fall to the wind or not heed sound advice and suffer injury. One may think he is above good counsel, overlook a gentle warning and sustain personal loss. Continual disregard of spiritual needs or guidelines for one's soul are detrimental to the well being of the Christian life. The consequences are lack of inner strength, a diminished spiritual life, and increasing inability to cope with difficult situations. Inability to cope leads to the disintegration of the personality.

One's life may break in the pursuit of an inflexible endeavor. Going one's own way, pushing forward regardless of the cost will lead to no good end. Advancing a project without consideration of a loved one's feelings or wishes causes harm to the self-esteem of the injured party. In that unswerving pursuit, one will scatter the broken fragments of love into a million pieces. And one's dreams of happiness are no more. Two lives, if not more, will have sustained serious personal injury.

One may also break friendships. Friends ought always to be appreciated. Friends trust us, believe in us, and most often are a very present help in trouble. But we must not take advantage of them or abuse them. It puts a strain on the relationship. Nor can we neglect them or take them for granted. Should we do so, we will leave friendships strewn and disintegrated about the community.

The Healing Waters of Grace

To keep our world from falling apart before our eyes, our lives must be endowed with an inner strength that shall be more than mere force. We must acquire the love of the Spirit that shall be stronger than fear, hate, or selfishness. And we must possess the fortitude that faith in Christ Jesus can bring to our lives. We cannot live well or successfully as broken bits of humanity. There must be oneness and wholeness to human lives.

To keep whole and to cease becoming fragmented, we must turn from self-absorption to Christ our Lord. There are three essential steps we can follow: 1) look to our Lord's love, grace, and sympathetic understanding, 2) alter attitudes and point of view, and 3) become open, understanding, and receptive. We are never so far along in our Christian walk that we cannot learn from the Master. His was a love that refused to sustain an injury. His was a love that never failed, even on a cross. His love held Simon Peter when Peter failed him and wept bitter tears. Our love must hope all things, believe all things, and endure all things. In endurance, we learn to be sympathetic. We will develop a harmony of feeling and mutual respect for one another. We will learn to share the feelings of another in sorrow or in trouble. In sharing their feelings we will come to understand their situation. And we can extend the same comfort wherewith we ourselves are comforted of God.

We will pray the Holy Spirit to help us alter our attitudes and point of view. We must not freeze our attitude or our mind, but pray for the grace to continue to grow and learn. William James once remarked, "The greatest discovery of my generation is that human beings can alter their lives by altering their attitudes of mind." When I attended my first ordination council, I distinctly remember an aged and retired minister standing and speaking to the candidate. "Young man, the most important thing in life and in your ministry is not the knowledge you may have acquired, nor the theology you may have accumulated in seminary, nor even the sequence and particulars of your beliefs, important as these may be. The most important thing, by far, will be your attitude of mind. You would always want to be receptive, understanding, and flexible. Don't freeze your attitude or your mind, but continue to grow and learn."

Going hand-in-hand with continuing to grow and learn is the need to have an open mind. We need not be closed to new or enlarged ideas in the application of the grace of our Lord Jesus Christ. I repeat again, our Savior's love can cover a multitude of sins. Our Gospel can meet the needs of all classes and conditions of men. It takes the love of our Lord Jesus to be receptive, and ought we not "let that mind which was in Christ Jesus also be in us"? In the end we need to have an open, receptive, and understanding mind if we are to understand fully the significance of our Savior's simple admonitions.

Gather Up the Fragments

Our Lord, who is the prince and author of life, does this for us. Not only can his Spirit open up our hearts to be receptive to his grace, but he can also open up our minds and enlarge our horizons. "To gather up the fragments that . . . nothing be lost" is a true mission of the Church. It is the ministry of reconciliation, it is salvation, and it is the Gospel. The significance of the word *repentance* is actually a turning of our outlook on life. It involves a new concept of the worth of things. It means seeking newer, deeper, and wider dimensions of life, and becoming part of a new and living way. Any life can be altered by altering one's attitude of mind. And the Spirit of the Lord Jesus can surely do this, as surely as he has altered the destiny of our souls.

As we unite in the worship in the presence of the consecrated elements, we are again reminded how necessary it is that we come to this encounter with our Lord with love, repentance, and faith, and with hearts that hunger and thirst for righteousness. This holy sacrament serves to remind us that we need our Savior's love and grace to keep us whole. We need his presence and Spirit to keep us from disintegrating under the stress and unpleasant incidents we encounter in life. Our sins of neglect have not left us uninjured or undamaged spiritually. His body that was broken for the love of us tells us that he can keep us from falling and from becoming fragmented. Our faith in the Lord Jesus gives meaning and purpose to our lives. In taking into our bodies the bread and wine, individuals are united in him, who is the author and finisher of life itself. The elements of bread and wine consecrated to holy use remind us of our oneness in Christ Jesus.

As we share in this holy sacrament, our Lord would lead us in the "more perfect way," enlarging our minds, hearts, and souls, in order that all the dimensions of life might be open to us. He would have us experience the unsearchable riches of his grace. But first, we must be capable of understanding and doing what these simple words of our Lord request: "Gather up the fragments that remain, that nothing be lost." Who would think of gathering up the fragments of the world's broken lives, lost loves, and shattered friendships? Only our Lord Jesus Christ and those who profess to love and follow him truly. Only those whom the Spirit has made sensitive to the world's hidden pain and anguish. The table of sacrament is a reminder that if we love the Lord Jesus, we will keep his commandments. His commandment is that we love one another, and that we "gather up the fragments that remain, that nothing be lost."

Prayer

Eternal Father, without Thee we have sensed our incompleteness, and our souls struggle to be at peace. Look down upon us, thy children, in mercy we pray Thee. And remember, O Lord our God, that we are thy people and the sheep of thy pasture. We stand in thy presence in need of forgiveness, that our individual burdens be lifted, that our yoke be made easy, and that we be encouraged in him who is for us the Way, the Truth, and the Life. May these consecrated elements of bread and wine speak to us of higher things. And may we leave Thy presence, knowing that we have been touched gently by Thy Spirit. Amen.

10

THE GRACE OF HOLY COMMUNION

We are gathered in the house of God to worship and adore our Redeemer who is present in his Spirit. The elements of Holy Communion attest to his coming among us once again. Physically, the Master does not walk our city streets, nor does he call us by name in a voice that can be heard above the unceasing press of life. Yet the Spirit speaks to the spirit and we feel the tugging of our souls. In the sacredness of this hour, by all that is holy and loved of God, let us truly consider our need of having our comfort and confidence renewed. Let our strength also be renewed in this our earthly pilgrimage. We come to receive from our heavenly Father the spirit of grace and supplication. And as we draw near the elements of bread and wine, may this heavenly grace deliver us from coldness of heart and wandering of mind. And thus, with steadfast thoughts and kindled spirits, may we worship in spirit and in truth.

It is not all that strange that Holy Communion has been held sacred by God's people since that first night in the Upper Room. In the most intimate hour of his earthly fellowship with the men God had given him, Christ instituted this holy sacrament as a gift of his grace. Among other things, it was meant to be a symbol of our Savior's presence among us forever. It is a token of his love for us and of God's love for us. It is a saving grace of reassurance to strengthen us as it was to strengthen the disciples for the worldwide task that lay ahead of them. Looking back on that first celebration, when this means of grace was instituted, the disciples of our Lord were in need of renewal. And having received the strength and assurance from our Savior's Spirit, they were to confess that the grace of our Lord Jesus Christ was sufficient for all their needs.

Wherever the call of God's Spirit was to send them, there they would experience the sustaining presence of their Lord. Whether it was witnessing for the great Galilean before kings or servants, or whether they were cast into prison for Christ's sake, they were comforted and strengthened by our Lord's abiding presence. Although Christ had ascended to the Father, his fellowship in the Spirit was a very real thing to the disciples. Whenever they could gather together or with the people to whom they ministered, upon the first day of the week, Holy Communion was found at the center of their worship service. And though the years had passed since the Last Supper, it was as though the Master sat among them as he had on the first night in the Upper Room. They could sense the warmth of his Spirit filling the sanctuary and pervading their bodies to the very root of their being.

They took to heart his words: "I shall not leave you comfortless: I will come to you" (John 14:18). The elements of the sacrament seemed to come to life, symbolizing his body that was broken for them and his blood that was shed for the remission of their sins. They could not help loving such a master, nor could they withhold from him the service of their lives. Simply to be in fellowship at the Lord's Supper was an enriching experience. They would recall the Master's words, his grief and compassion, and his message of assurance, "Let not your heart be troubled, neither let it be afraid." You believe in God, believe also in me (John 14:27).

The disciples had poignant reasons for troubled hearts. Their Lord had been taken away, they had lost James to the edge of the sword, and the authorities sought to destroy the fellowship. Most men would have hesitated and others would have turned back, shackled by fear. But the Master had promised and had given them a commission to the uttermost parts of the world. Even there Jesus would be with them. This promise of Christ, "Lo, I am with you always," (Matt. 28:20) was made real and present to them in the sacrament of Holy Communion. The disciples came to the elements with knowledge, faith, repentance, and love, and with hearts that hungered for his presence. Having confessed their need of strength and comfort, they were renewed. They were strengthened with might through our Savior's spirit in the inner man. Amidst the perplexities and dangers of their times, the disciples of our Lord could leave the sacramental table, saying: "For me to live is Christ (Phil. 1:21) . . . I can do all things through Christ which strengtheneth me (Phil. 4:13) . . . We are more than conquerors through Jesus Christ who loved us" (Rom. 8:37).

They, like we, had come to worship and adore the Lord, with hearts that troubled them, minds confused, and tired bodies. Without were the clamor of the battle, the noise of the milling multitude, and the watchful eye of the chief priest. Their spirits were restless. They needed to recall his promise and words of assurance: "Peace I leave with you, my peace I give unto you: not as the world giveth, give I unto you . . . Let not your heart be troubled, neither let it be afraid" (John 14:27). They came to the sacramental table faint of soul and exhausted of spirit, and when they departed their several ways they went forth to conquer in the name of the Galilean. What was their secret? They had been in the presence of Jesus Christ. They had supped with the Master and were filled with the fullness of God.

At the communion hour our Master once again extends his summons, and we come at his invitation of grace confessing our need of him. His one wish is that Holy Communion be a true sacrament to us. He has not fallen back on his word or altered the thing that has gone out of his mouth. He comes to us with the same promise and with the same words, "Lo, I am with you always . . . Peace I give unto you . . . Let not your heart be troubled, neither let it be afraid." This is an age of troubled hearts the world over, of spirits that are bowed and broken, of bodies that are racked with pain, and of minds beset with woe. Our nation is troubled, the people are troubled, and all seek rest for their souls and peace for their hearts. Amid the turmoil and conflicting tendencies that scream to be heard, there has evolved a confusion of tongues and the people are divided one from another. One scarcely knows what is worth believing, what one can lay hold of and trust upon in all this babble of voices.

We are troubled because we live in an era of wonder, confusion, and nondirection. We have unleashed a power that the prophets could never have dreamed of. We have probed deeper into the sea with every passing year and every month we hear of new wonders in medicine. As a nation and as individuals we possess more wealth than ever before, and still there is vast poverty and suffering among our people. But our prosperity is no mean thing. No wonder we are confused and disturbed.

We have far outreached our capacity in spirit to deal with all the wonders and power of this age. The very possibility that the power for peace that we have created may turn into an uncontrolled monster of vast destruction frightens us. We spend billions for defense and for foreign aid, and we are incapable of solving the problems of poverty, health care, and suffering within our own borders. Our spirits have reason to be faint.

In sympathetic understanding, our Savior calls us in from the noise and strife of the world, because without faith in God and the assurance that our Lord is still sovereign, the tensions of life would snap our minds like tightly wound guitar strings. If left utterly to ourselves, our souls would be crushed under the burden. Without God's love and grace our spirits would surely die. And so, we have come to be renewed and strengthened; we have come to be blessed by our Savior's grace; we have come to confess our faults, failures, and sins; we have come because we felt harried by the world; and we have come because we want to be immersed in his life-giving presence. We have gathered at this table because we need each other's fellowship as our individual bodies need their several members. We have come to find quiet for our souls, that our Master's peace might still the tempest that periodically rages within us.

May Holy Communion be efficacious for our every need. The difficulties that beset us, the secret anguish of our hearts, the hidden pain we bear are all covered over by the body and blood of our Savior. He will bless us. He will help us, and no good thing will be withheld from those that love him and seek him with their whole hearts. Secretly, we may have our own separate crosses, and when we leave this sanctuary, we go our individual ways, but all crosses and all ways become one as in penitent belief we make ready to receive the Lord's Supper. Our Redeemer comes to us with a saving grace that knows no measure and is not stopped by any power on Earth or heaven, but that seeks and finds, that comforts and redeems.

In this fellowship of grace, the love from God overflows from heart to heart among those who love his Son, and the Body of Christ is strengthened. Like the members of the early Church, we can leave the house of worship knowing that we have been in the presence of Christ and knowing that we have been fed from heaven. We can echo in spirit with those who have held high the banner of the Church in ages past: "For me to live in Christ . . . I can do all things through Christ who strengtheneth me . . . we are more than conquerors through Christ Jesus who loved us." For "of his fullness we have all received, grace for grace" (John 1:16).

Prayer

O Lord our God, Thou only hast consecrated for thy people a new and living way, Jesus Christ our Lord. As we take into our bodies this bread and wine, may our lives yield to the touch of his Spirit. In partaking of this holy institution we are aware that we commemorate our Savior's Last Supper with his disciples and his offering of himself in the sacrifice of the cross. Eternal Father, grant thy Holy Spirit that the bread and wine become for us the body that was broken and the blood that was shed for us. And as we receive this holy sacrament to our comfort, may they work in us penitent hearts and quickened spirits. Amen.

11

Holy Communion:
The Christian Dynamic

T
here are times when we wonder where we are going to acquire the energy and drive to sustain our way in life? Some days we are worn and exhausted by work, by the children, by sickness, by any number of things. Our spiritual life also appears to have been expended and we lack the energy to revive our souls. There is a passage of Scripture that applies to times like these:

> that you might . . . know what is the immeasurable greatness of his power in us who believe, according to the working of his great might which he accomplished in Christ when he raised him from the dead and made him sit at his right hand in heavenly places. (Eph. 1:19–20)

In Ibsen's play, *The Emperor and the Galilean*, Julian the apostate exclaimed:

> You cannot comprehend it, thou who has never been under the power of the God-man. It is more than teaching that he spreads over the earth: it must be witchcraft that takes the mind captive. There is a vast power there. And they who have been under his influence, I believe, can never get free.

The sufficiency of the Christian faith and life resides in the greatness of God's power, and we attribute ultimate power only to God and to our Lord Jesus Christ.

Spiritual Energy Comes From God

We all need a power, a dynamic force that will enable us to cope with the mystery of existence. We are in need of a source of energy that can bring us to a better state in life, lift us up, and sustain us. We are reminded that spiritual power is precisely what we have in our concept of religious faith. In Christ our Lord there is power to uplift, to make us aspire to the higher things in life, and to restore us to fellowship with God. The power and influence of Christianity are unending and dynamic.

A thing that is dynamic is characterized by forceful movement. From the beginning of Christianity as a world religion, it was characterized by the impelling growth of its influence and its conquest of the human soul. The New Testament writers attributed this phenomenon to the power of God, which was intrinsic in the new faith. This idea may seem strange and a bit alien to us, because it is difficult for us to imagine ourselves infused with the power and energy of The Almighty. Moreover, when weary from the struggles of life, we lose the energy necessary to deal with the issues that confront us. And the thought that a dynamic force resides in us is difficult to accept. To a people that were worn, weary, and exhausted, Isaiah wrote:

> The Lord, the creator of the ends of the earth fainteth not, neither is he weary. There is no searching of his understanding. He giveth power to the faint; and to them that have no might, he increaseth strength. (Is. 40:28, 29)

When we say that creative power and spiritual energy are intrinsic to the Christian religion, we mean that they are inherent in our faith, belonging to our expression of belief and worship, apart from the circumstances that may affect our personal estimate of it. When Isaiah the prophet proclaimed the creative might of God's power to the nation of Israel, they as a people had suffered greatly. Their kingdom had been ravaged by aggressive military powers, by civil conflict, by famine and drought. Their population had vastly diminished, and what little energy remained to the nation was dissipated in a constant struggle for survival. The prevalent belief of the surrounding nations was that the power and strength of a people reflected the power and ability of their God.

Isaiah directed their thoughts away from their present circumstances, away from the concepts expressed in the worldly empires around them, and to the Lord God. The Lord God, the creator of heaven and earth, had also created them as a nation.

Today, many of the pews in a vast number of churches are empty. Growth in membership, power, and influence appears curtailed. The moral impact of the Church seems inert. The high ethical and moral principles once germane and attributed to Christianity are in conflict with a permissive, expressive society where anything goes. Crime in the cities, violence in the streets, and murder in the home are all around us. We may question, with the weight of the circumstances that appear to affect our perspective, whether the effectiveness of Christianity is running down. Have the centuries drained its force for good, and has its redemptive power in society and the individual diminished? While it may appear that the force and influence of Christianity has lessened, the appearance is only an illusion. Creative power is inherent to the Christian religion, and the God whom we worship is an unending source of spiritual energy. When an individual turns to the Lord Jesus, the Holy Spirit is still able to transform that life and work a new creation. When we think about the force and effectiveness of our religion, we look, with the prophet Isaiah, to the Lord God, creator of heaven and Earth.

The Witness of the Sacrament of Holy Communion

In Holy Communion, the elements of bread and wine give witness to our common belief. We may be unable to answer for the spiritual and moral condition of the world at large, but the sacrament of Holy Communion does. It gives testimony against the world's violence, hate, and moral fault. It testifies against its alien spirit, which is in rebellion against God and his righteousness. But the sacrament also gives witness to the way to righteousness and to the power of the Christian religion, to the power of our Lord's resurrection. We come to the sacrament because we know that our Savior's presence imparts a forceful spiritual grace. We need this grace to sustain our spiritual life and our union with Christ.

We are invited to believe that God in Christ Jesus can supply the creative energy necessary to a good mental, moral, and spiritual life. The forceful impetus of the Christian religion, which works upon the soul, rests in the greatness of God's compassion. The enduring quality of our expression of worship lies in the gentleness and ability of the Holy Spirit's power for renewal. It is precisely for this reason that we come to the sacramental table. We seek fortitude of spirit as we partake of the consecrated bread and wine. We come to rest for a moment under the shadow of our great Rock, to be enriched and infused with our Lord's grace and strength.

But we must come, believe, and worship. We come to be apart from all the confusion, distress, conflict, and turmoil involved in the circumstances of the outside world. We come to be a part of the testimony, with that great company of unseen witnesses who have gone before us, that it is our faith to believe in God and in Jesus Christ his Son. The witness of the sacrament is that God was in Christ reconciling the world unto himself and we come to be identified with this movement. What made Christianity such a forceful movement in its initial stages was the revelation that one could have a meaningful life when related to God and the hope of immortality that our Savior brought to a dying world. The sacrament of Holy Communion is a revelation to the world by its continuity to witness to our Lord's love and sacrifice, to his resurrection, and by continuing to give grace and spiritual strength to the communicant, that a life lived in nearness to God is never devoid of meaning or purpose; and that because we accept the eternity of God, our hope of immortality is grounded in him.

Julian said that one could not comprehend the attraction of Christianity as a movement, nor of the power of the God-man to draw others "unto himself." From the viewpoint of a world ruler, he saw a vast power, a dynamic force that sprang from the Christian religion, and he likened it to an unknown influence that took the mind captive. The emperor Julian, who once had professed Christ, saw the evidence of the deep effectiveness of the Christian religion as it worked in the life of the individual; and he thought it to be incomprehensible. The apostle Paul wanted us to know or to imagine the greatness and potential inherent in Christianity. He pointed to the Savior's resurrection through which God the creator demonstrated the greatness of his power and purpose. We worship a risen and living Lord, and to this cardinal tenet of our faith, these elements of bread and wine testify; and they testify also to the immeasurable greatness of the vast, eternal power that brought this about. And, however strengthened we may feel when we leave the sanctuary, this energy is only a tiny aspect of God's power.

All the promises of our religion, its hope and expectation for the future and what they mean for us personally, are focused in the sacrament of Holy Communion. It was our Lord's resurrection that set the seal on his teaching, person, and promises. What the Almighty has promised in the expression of his benevolence, he will accomplish in his providence. God demonstrated his ability to do so when he raised Jesus from the dead. As this applies to us, the meaning is this: the hidden sorrow, the ills that may affect our bodies, and even the propensity to doubt, can all be resolved in the healing waters of God's grace, which is offered to us in Holy Communion. Where we are in the progress of our religious life is of no impeding consequences and what our individual needs may be are of no difficulty to our Lord's ability. The Lord of the ages is able to reach out to all that seek his presence.

The Wonder of This Power May Reside in Us

The thought that Paul conveyed, when he wrote about the power of God, was that the dynamic force of the Christian religion may reside in us individually: "That you might know what is the immeasurable greatness of his power in us."

We have reason to wonder at the thought, *is the power of God that upholds the vast universe or any small part of it actually in us?* Is the eternal, creative energy that made the worlds available to us? St. Paul said, yes, it is actually so. God who made the worlds has placed the power of his Spirit in us and made us the recipients of his benevolence. When we turn to the Lord Jesus, the uplifting influence of his presence, the spiritual energy that can bring us nearer to what God intended us to be, is awakened in our inner being. The real wonder is that when we have turned to the Lord Jesus, it is there, and it is present in us whether or not we acknowledge it, are aware of it, or use it.

With many believers, this power lies latent, while others doubt the actual reality of the influence of God's Spirit in us. But to doubt is simply to waver in opinion or to be undecided. Most nearly, it means to be unsettled in the belief as to the reality of a thing and the reason is lack of certainty. Credibility may be enhanced through knowledge or personal experience. The forceful movement of Christianity, its transforming ability, is germane to its nature and the main work it seeks to do in the life of an individual, apart from what anyone may say or think about it. It is internal to the wonder and mystery of the faith and love that are in Christ Jesus. When we turn to the Lord Jesus, the transforming, unseen work of the Holy Spirit is well begun.

Looking to the Christ of the cross, or going through the confirmation process, is a personal experience. Somewhere along in the process, thoughts cross our minds, our feelings are stirred, and our hearts moved. We make our confession of faith in Christ Jesus, and some individuals in making this confession are moved a great deal. Before he became the chief advocate of the Christian religion, Paul was aware of the claims of Christ and the teachings of the new religion. He wished to impede its growth, not believing in it or in its claim of divine energy, direction, and spirit. But his personal encounter with the risen Christ changed his character, attitude, and thinking. He also changed quite drastically his concept about the power of the Christian faith, as it was exemplified in Christ Jesus. The forceful and creative nature of his own religious life and work removed any unsettled beliefs he may have had about the power of God expressed through the Christian religion. Once his doubts vanished, Paul never questioned the divine energy and strength inherent in the faith he embraced. Time and time again, when in need, he appealed to Christ for strength, for deliverance, and effectiveness in his life's work. Having discovered this marvelous, unseen, hidden source of energy, never more did it remain unused, untapped, and unexercised.

We may not be blessed with such a sudden and dramatic encounter with the risen Lord Jesus as experienced by the apostle Paul. Yet he whom we worship speaks to us, touches our hearts, hears, and answers our prayers. If not yet, then some day, in answer to our prayers, we will sense the Savior's presence; it may be as though it came on the breath of a soft spring morning. We will have obtained the certainty that the power of grace has touched our lives, and that Christ's Spirit resides in us. In the mystery of the dispensation of God's providence, this can be true for all that claim the gentle Jesus as Savior and Lord. Meanwhile, we can mediate on these things as we gather about the sacrament of Holy Communion where the bread of life is broken for us. Together we testify to our Lord's sacrifice and to the power of his resurrection. Here before us is the image, symbol, and present reality of our spiritual life, its renewal, and enduring power of the Christian faith. This is God's gift to us. Ours is but to believe, receive, embrace the promise, and avail ourselves of its benefits. We can do so as we take the bread and wine into our bodies. Amen.

12

THE UPPER ROOM

It was in the last days of the first Lenten season. The Passion of our Lord has just begun, and the disciples of our Lord were disturbed and uncertain. They did not know what lay ahead. The times were troubled. There were doubts and suspicions abroad. Our Lord planned to go to the Garden to be strengthened for the ordeal of the cross. Already, in the mind of the chief priest, the death of the Lord Christ Jesus was certain. The plot against Jesus' life already hatched, need only to be carried out by the temple agents. The unspoken thoughts of those who plotted the death of the Christ of God were, *Smite the shepherd and the flock will scatter*. And so, the plotters believed, this movement of the Way would cease.

The time was late evening, for night was falling. The night would obscure the watchful eyes of informers. The people coming and going were fewer, and only those who needed to be out traversed through the night. It was also much quieter. The shops and the market place were shut down, and much of the city was at the evening meal. The gathering of our Lord with his disciples would scarcely attract any notice. This set well with the Master. Jesus wanted to be alone for a short while with his disciples. It was no time for the intrusion of the world or worldly noises.

The place was an obscure upper room of a building, set away from the main avenues of the city. Here Jesus met with his disciples to share the evening Passover meal. This meal in the Upper Room would be their last hour with the Master. It was here at the Last Supper, united in fellowship with his disciples, that Christ our Lord set before them the elements of bread and wine. Here, in the Upper Room, the Lord Jesus instituted the sacrament of Holy Communion. And here, also, it would be a time when the Savior would give his disciples the strength, comfort, and hope of his spiritual efficacy. Our Lord knew what they had need of. Their hearts were troubled.

As the events would prove, the disciples were to need all the strength and endurance that God would give them. Their Lord was to be taken from them, but while he yet remained with them Jesus wanted to give them hope. The Lord Jesus wanted to comfort them and encourage them in the way they had chosen. He wanted them to remember their times together, the things of God he had taught them, and the way of the kingdom of heaven. He wanted them to know that while the world might despise them, God loved them, and Jesus loved them enough to give his life for them. Thus, the disciples came together to join with their Lord Jesus for the Last Supper in the Upper Room.

Hearts are always troubled in troubled times. Even today, our fears, anxieties, and sins are no different from those of other times, nor from those of the disciples. To us, also, our Lord extends his invitation to come and sup with him in order that we might partake of the heavenly manna. The sacrament of Holy Communion is an undying source of spiritual comfort for the Church of Jesus Christ. It can be as real and sufficient for us as it has been for God's people in all times and as it was for the disciples of our Lord in that Upper Room of long ago.

A Means of Grace

This sacrament is to us a means of grace, an instrument through which God imparts the blessings of his mercy. God blesses, and his Spirit is active towards us in this sacrament as in no other ministry of the church. God can bless in many ways, with good health, goodly children, and with peace and prosperity. But the sacrament of Holy Communion is God's appointed way of blessing and of speaking to the human soul. This is precisely why we come to have our souls blessed with God's Spirit and love. These elements of bread and wine are God's food for our souls and their spiritual growth; they are to us the saving body and blood of Christ.

A Pledge of Renewal

When the disciples met with their Lord in the Upper Room, the very first words that Jesus spoke to them were these:

> Let not your heart be troubled: you believe in God, believe also in me. (John 14:1)

These words were meant also for us. Christ our Lord, as our High Priest, is offering to us the reconciliating grace of his body and blood as a pledge of renewal. We have his solemn promise to restore to our souls that which the events of life may have taken from us and to replenish our spiritual want. God alone knows how much we need the daily renewal of his mercies, and it is in spiritual renewal that we find the strength of the Christian faith. This may appear hidden from so many because it seems so simple a means, and so is faith. Nevertheless, the strength of the Christian faith is in renewal. That night the disciples were in need of strength. Jesus offered it to them during that first Holy Communion. And the Lord Jesus offers that same strength to us in our hour of fellowship with him.

We may feel that our body, because of age or infirmity, is incapable of generating much strength. But with Jesus Christ our weakness is made strong. The Savior can strengthen our spirit, and our spirit is that entity in us that sustains our Christian life, our affinity with Christ, and all that the Christian religion means to us. As we wait on our Lord in the presence of the consecrated bread and wine, let us remember that, "They that wait upon the Lord, shall renew their strength," (Is. 40:31) and they shall mount up on the wings of the Spirit like an eagle.

A Pledge of Comfort

While this service is a pledge of renewal and strength, it is also a pledge of comfort. As we unite in worship and praise, the comfort of God is shed abroad in our hearts. In times of trouble and anguish of heart, Isaiah led the people to look to the mercy and comfort of God: "Comfort ye, comfort ye my people, saith your God. Speak ye comfortably to Jerusalem" (Is. 40:1, 2). In unity with the words of the prophet Isaiah, the apostle Paul, thinking on the comfort of God, expressed his gratitude:

> Blessed be God, even the Father of our Lord Jesus Christ, the Father of mercies, and the God of all comfort; Who comforts us in all our tribulations. (2 Cor. 1:3, 4)

The troubled of heart need more than strength. They need the assurance and comfort of God's love. Jesus took the occasion of the Last Supper to comfort his disciples with the assurance of his love for them. Knowing that after he was taken away, they would be lonely, indecisive, and disquieted, the Lord Jesus gave them this promise:

> And I will pray the Father, and he shall give you another Comforter, that he may abide with you forever. (John 14:16)

What a marvelous grace was revealed that night. At the first Holy Communion, the promise of the Holy Spirit as the Comforter was given. And as often as we eat this bread and drink this wine, that promise is renewed to the Church of Jesus Christ. It is as though in communion with the Holy Spirit, our Lord comes to assure us of the comfort and love of God. He brings to troubled hearts rest, assurance, and peace, with "the comfort wherewith we ourselves are comforted of God" (2 Cor. 1:4).

The Holy Spirit Gives Hope

To those troubled disciples in the Upper Room, our Lord gave three things: strength, comfort, and hope. Here, amidst the elements of bread and wine, our Lord brings these same spiritual realities to us as we share in the table of sacrament. Here we receive strength through the renewal of our spiritual life, comfort through the assurance of God's love and care, and hope through the Holy Spirit. Hope is the expectation that what we desire will occur. We hope because we have faith. And with faith and patience we can wait for our expectations to be realized. Our hope is in the Lord Jesus Christ, and we hope through the Spirit, which God gave to the Church of Jesus Christ. And hope resides in us as a permanent gift of God the Father of our spirits.

It is the Holy Spirit that first called us to the cross and to the Lord Jesus and to the redemption that is in him. He called us to grace and glory; and at some future time, the Holy Spirit will call us to life everlasting. The ultimate hope of the Christian faith is our spiritual consummation with God and our Lord Jesus Christ in the new heaven and the new earth. Our Lord's words of truth and grace are these:

> In my Father's house there are many mansions; if it were not so, I would have told you. I go to prepare a place for you. And if I go and prepare a place for you, I will come again, and receive you unto myself; that where I am, there you may be also. (John 14:2–3)

We acknowledge the presence of our Redeemer as we worship in his name, and he comes to strengthen, comfort, and encourage us in our faith. But we must come to this table, and we must eat of the bread and drink of the cup, and we must do so in the hope of our faith. We must come with the thought of repentance, with gratitude for God's forgiveness, and with praise. We come for absolution and assurance, and we come with the prayers of thanksgiving. And if we are sincere and of a contrite heart, the Lord Jesus will receive us unto himself. Amen.

13

A MOMENT OF RETROSPECTION

Reminding the Corinthians of how he had received from the Lord Jesus the sacrament of Holy Communion, St. Paul wrote:

Wherefore whosoever shall eat this bread, and drink this cup of the Lord unworthily, shall be guilty of the body and blood of the Lord. But let a man examine himself, and so let him eat of that bread, and drink of that cup. (1 Cor. 11:27, 28)

These words of St. Paul introduce our thought for this occasion, "But let a man examine himself, and so let him eat of that bread, and drink of that cup."

A Moment of Retrospection

Amidst holy things and in the presence of the eternal Spirit we are united in worship, and our Redeemer has called us to partake of the symbols of his body and blood. We do so in remembrance of his devotion and sacrifice on our behalf. Our Lord's desire is that we may be spiritually enriched through the observance of this sacrament. But we are in danger of betraying him, of letting the significance of this moment slip through our minds. We are cautioned not to profane the body and blood of our Lord by eating the bread and drinking the cup in an unworthy manner. Thus we pause for a moment of retrospection, during which we seek to examine ourselves. We seek to cleanse and rededicate ourselves once again to the cause of Christ Jesus.

Though we may be reluctant to take a close look at ourselves, our Lord stressed the self-examined life when he said, "And why beholdest thou the mote that is in thy brother's eye, but considerest not the beam that is in thine own eye?" (Matt. 7:3). Was the Master's perception not true? We readily see the faults of others, while so easily overlooking our own shortcomings. The Lord Jesus told the parable about two men who went to the temple to pray. One stood erect, head held high, shoulders back, proud in his stature, and said, "Father, I thank thee that I am not as other men." The other man stood with his head held low, and in a penitent supplication uttered, "God be merciful to me a sinner" (Luke 18:13). In making his evaluation of these two revelations of self-examination, our Master said that the penitent publican had alone been justified in the presence of God. One had looked at himself as though looking through a mist and saw only what he thought would be good to reveal. The second man looked, examined himself frankly, and acknowledged the truth of what he saw. He knew his state. He knew in his heart that he could only stand in God's presence when he was enabled to admit his human frailty. In like manner, we may come into God's presence, seeking his love, absolution, and acceptance.

Long before the first advent of our Lord, a Greek sage taught that it was unworthy of man to live an unexamined life. He pointed out that the outer man must be brought into conformity with the inner, spiritual man. Our retrospection begins with an examination of our thoughts and leads to a scrutiny of our acts. It ought to embrace our whole lives. "As a man thinketh in his heart, so is he" (Prov. 23:7). We recognize that evil may lurk in the heart. But there is also much that is good and noble residing in the soul of man. The question is which shall be controlling, the evil or the good?

Which shall guide our thoughts, motives, and the direction of our lives?

Hidden in our thoughts are dreams yet to be realized, secret hopes and ambitions that we have not brought to fruition. Embedded there are also our sorrows, tears, and pains. From these thoughts and emotions spring our actions. Actions are the things we do. They are also the scowl or smile on our face. They are the love we share or hold back, and they are the gifts we receive and those we give. No one but God and we know the thoughts and motives behind our acts. And we are bidden to take an honest look at ourselves and to determine whether we have the courage to live with an examined life and so share in the communion of our Lord's table.

The Cleansing of Our Souls

When Moses drew near the burning bush to see what caused this strange and wonderful sight, he was given notice that he was walking on holy ground. He was made aware that he was in the presence of The Almighty. About this sacramental table we also are on holy ground and in the presence of The Almighty. We come seeking our Savior's cleansing grace in order to approach his presence. And this affects the disposition of the heart. St. Paul wrote to the church in Ephesus, saying:

> Let all bitterness, and wrath, and anger, and clamour, and evil speaking be put away from you, with all malice: And be you kind one to another, tender-hearted, forgiving one another, even as God for Christ's sake hath forgiven you. (Eph. 4:31, 32)

With the apostle Paul, all the above we seek to put away from us before we take into our bodies the bread and wine. But when we consider man's inhumanity to man, his crimes, wars, and suppressions, we are inclined to ask, "How can these things be? How can man be made clean in the sight of God?" When Lady Macbeth tried to wash the bloodstains from her hands after she had murdered, she was unable to do so. No matter how hard she tried to remove them, the spots remained. It was not so much because her hands were spotted, but because her soul had been stained and her heart darkened. Our need is for a pure and contrite heart. Grace must touch our souls.

When the prophet Isaiah received the vision of God in the temple, he fell back in anguish and despair, saying: "Woe is me for I am undone:" (Is. 6:5). I am soiled, and I have come into the presence of The Almighty. Then one of the angels near the throne of grace took a live coal from the altar and came and touched the lips of Isaiah, saying, "Be thou clean." Grace can cleanse the heart and heal the soul. The Lord God is cognizant of our need, and in his grace he gives what he commands in his holiness. When we lift the cup to our lips, remember the words of the Savior, "thy sins are forgiven thee" (Luke 5:20). When confessing our sins, God is "Just and faithful to forgive us our sins: and to cleanse us from all unrighteousness" (1 John 1:9). God's grace enables us to come into his presence. As the spiritual influence is sensed among us, we welcome the grace, love, and power of God in our lives that we might obtain mercy and be cleansed from all unrighteousness.

As we partake of the elements of bread and wine, our hearts are touched by the love that will not let us go nor leave us to ourselves. We are made aware that Christ is present with us about this table in all the power of his uplifting Spirit. While we may not see him, we sense and feel the assurance of his communion and love. When we will have left this sanctuary, we will have come to understand that God has called us to be his people and that he has anointed us with the Holy Spirit.

A Deeper Dedication

This moment of retrospection enables us to confess our sins and to cleanse our souls through spiritual communion. It also calls us to a deeper sense of dedication. If our nation and people suffer from lack of anything, it is from lack of dedication. Modern man may wonder what is there to which he may dedicate himself. We tend to be blown about by every wandering wind. At times, we are not sure whether it is spiritual weakness or timidity that keeps us back. Still, we need something, some vision or ideal, or some cause to which we can anchor our souls. That ideal is Christ himself.

A monument has been erected to the men of a wrecked ship. At the cost of their lives they endeavored to save their passengers. But everyone drowned. The only bodies washed ashore were those of the passengers who wore life belts. There had not been enough life belts for everyone and the men had chosen to go without them. These men were dedicated to the tradition of the sea. Ought we not to be dedicated to the cause of Christ our Lord? As we eat this bread and drink this cup, let us recall our need for self-examination. Let us dwell on the cleansing power of the Holy Spirit, and let us dedicate ourselves anew to our God and Savior Jesus Christ.

14

A MEMORIAL OF LOVE
AND DEVOTION

When Spring is near and sunlight lengthens, the days begin to warm and our hearts are made glad. Spring is the harbinger of the season of Lent, when the meaning of the cross will be on our minds. Faith, hope, and love become more expressive in our religious life, as we sense the unfolding of the mystery of godliness. These are the days when the Spirit of God manifests his visitation in the hearts of the people. Witnessed by the elements of bread and wine, we have before us a memorial of love and devotion.

A memorial is an event that helps us to remember someone or some event of the past. The Lord Jesus directed a memorial to Mary Magdalene because of the deep affection that she displayed for the Savior; and since Mary had been forgiven much, she loved the Lord Jesus all the more. Her devotion was seen in an earnest dedication to the cause of Christ.

> Now when Jesus was in Bethany, in the house of Simon the leper, there came a woman [Mary Magdalene], having an alabaster box of very precious ointment, and poured it on his head. (Matt 26:6–7)

Mary was chided for what some of the Lord's disciples thought to be an act of utter waste. But our Lord silenced them, saying:

> Why trouble ye this woman? for she hath wrought a good work upon me . . . For in that she hath poured this ointment on my body, she did it for my burial. (Matt 26:10, 12)

It was some time later that Jesus spoke of his life, mission, and death. He saw his life given as a "ransom for many" and for their salvation. He spoke of this ministry of love and self-sacrifice in the Upper Room during the Last Supper, when he instituted the sacrament of Holy Communion. It was this conception of his life and work which was revealed to Mary Magdalene and to which she gave witness, when she poured over the Lord Jesus the precious ointment. This concept of Christ's ministry was the foundation on which the early fellowship of believers was established, and on which the Church of Jesus Christ was built. Our Lord's life, death, and resurrection are the subjects of our preaching, worship, and the Gospel of the church. In the presence of the disciples, when Mary poured the ointment over Jesus, it was an expression of her dedication to his mission. She had done it, said our Lord, "against the day of my burying."

Mary Expressed Faith, Hope, and Love

With Mary, her act, while touched with sorrow, revealed her faith, hope, and love in the Lord Jesus. Our Lord was aware of this, because from the beginning he knew those who would remain faithful. The Lord Jesus affirmed that wherever the Gospel would be preached, her act would be deemed a memorial for her. From the depths of her soul, it was an act impelled by her intense belief in Jesus, who had redeemed her soul and brought her into the kingdom of heaven. If any individual had been given a new life, it was Mary Magdalene. She believed in him, nothing doubting, and accepted our Lord's words of truth and grace. She poured the ointment over his head and feet, and then wiped them with her hair, and her act became Mary's confession of unity with Christ and with his cross. As Mary had united with the Lord Jesus in his life, she was also united with him in his death and resurrection.

This was a wonderful expression of faith in the Christ of God to have been made by Mary, and only Jesus recognized it. In this confession, she stood with her Savior, and it appeared that she alone of all those who professed to follow Jesus, including his disciples, had accepted our Lord's death and burial. Jesus knew it and loved her for that. Later, on that bright resurrection morning, Mary would ask, "Where have you taken my Lord?" Where, indeed! Was it any wonder that Jesus said to his disciples, this will be "a memorial for her" (Matt 26:13)? This is also true of many who confess the Lord Jesus today; in times of meditation, or prayer, there will be moments when the Savior's presence will be sensed to be near, and we will feel as though we stand alone with our Lord, like Mary Magdalene.

The Memorial to Our Lord

In coming to the table of sacrament, we celebrate a memorial of our Lord's love and devotion. It is so for all who look to the Lord Jesus with faith, hope, and love. Holy Communion is deemed a memorial to our Savior's love and self-giving, and this is true wherever the Gospel is preached. Is it not true that the first thing that we know about the Lord Jesus is that he loved us and gave himself for us? Our being here expresses our confession in Christ Jesus. When Mary anointed our Lord with the precious ointment, it was more than an act of dedication to his mission; she was trusting the Lord Jesus with the destiny of her soul. Our presence around the sacramental table expressed the same sentiments, as did Mary. As we share in the simple elements of bread and wine, we witness our devotion to Christ until he comes, and this is a response that we make to the presence of the Spirit of our Lord and to our fellowship in worship.

A Memorial to the Women of Our Faith

Mary Magdalene was not the only woman who responded to the manifestation of God's love and grace. Since the birth of our faith, our women have always shown their affection for the king-dom of God. From the Old Testament narrative we learn that Hannah was barren. She prayed for a son, and the prayer was granted. When weaned, she gave the child to the Lord. All the days of his life that child was lent to the Lord God. That child, Samuel, was the beginning of the prophetic office in Israel. Hannah's response, like that of Mary, came from her soul:

> My heart is made strong in the Lord, and my horn is exalted in my God: because none is holy as the Lord: I am made glad in thy salvation; and none is righteous as our God. For a God of knowl-edge is the Lord, and a God preparing his curious design. The bow of the mighty he hath made weak, and the weak are girded with strength. . . For the barren hath born seven . . . The Lord killeth and maketh alive: he bringeth down to hell, and bringeth up again. He raiseth up the poor out of the dust that he might set among the mighty; and he hath blessed the years of the just: for man is not mighty in strength. (1 Sam. 2:1–10)

Our Devotion

Holy Communion was meant to encourage us in our religious life and to evoke a response in worship. In this devotional setting, we seek to awaken a spiritual affection toward Christ our Lord, and God our Father. We come to enhance our spiritual life. We come to make ready our hearts and souls to encounter the Spirit of the Eternal, and as we address God in words of prayer and thanks-giving, our thoughts ascend to God. Our prayers and praise as-cend to the only King eternal, invisible, who alone divides the day from the darkness, and who alone can turn the shadows of night into the bright morning of his grace and presence.

As we make ready to receive the consecrated elements of bread and wine, we pray the Lord God may incline our hearts to keep his ways; for indeed, God must turn us to himself. St. Augustine prayed:

> How can we turn to Thee, O Lord our God, unless in mercy Thou dost turn us unto Thyself . . . For Thou only art my glory,

O Lord, and The Lifter up of my head. Thou only has redeemed my soul from destruction. (St. Augustine, Confession)

Sharing in this memorial of self-giving love, we pray for God's blessing on all that worship him. We pray that grace may touch our lives, for God's goodness upon us, and for the inspiration of his love. We pray for reception into his presence, now and forever. In devotion to our Lord, we would learn to suffer long, one with another, and that all our acts be touched with kindness. In spite of all human tendencies to the contrary, we pray that faith, hope, and love never die out in the expression of our religious life. We come to this sacrament because we are made glad in God's salvation, and because none is holy like the Lord, we pray that our affection for him will be sincere. As with Hannah and Mary Magdalene, we pray that our devotion may bear all things, that we believe all things and hope all things. Amen.

15

BEHOLD, I SHOW YOU
A MYSTERY

Generally, we celebrate the sacrament of Holy Communion every month. But there is a danger that we may overlook all that it means to our religious life. Unless we refresh our memories, we may pass over some elements of its witness. The Christian church has a two thousand-year history. Its roots springing out of the Old Testament, go back several thousand years beyond the Christian era, when Christ was born in the province of Judea. Our expression of worship, with rich volumes of literature and inspirational music, has grown out of a tradition nurtured though lives of self-sacrifice.

The influence of the Christian religion has not only affected human life for good, but has also laid a good foundation for art, drama, and literature. Modern drama began with plays on the Passion of our Lord. The greatest paintings and works of sculpture in Western civilization were created with a religious theme. And we doubt whether any written work can match the literary expression, the beauty of symmetry and balance contained in *The Authorized Version of the Scriptures*. As long as men and women feel the need of God, and as long as men and women seek solace for their souls, that need and consolation will surely be expressed in works of art, literature, and drama. Men and women give expression to their thoughts and feelings, when moved by a religious impulse, because our faith speaks to the human heart, and because it responds to the need of the soul. The sacrament of Holy Communion both speaks to the human heart and responds to the need of the human soul.

The Drama of Holy Communion

Holy Communion is a religious drama. The sacrament is a composition in prose and elements, presenting in the communion of the bread and wine the story of our Lord's Passion. It dramatizes our Lord's love and his sacrifice on the cross. The congregation is not a mere spectator, but a vital participant in the worship service of the bread and wine. The drama of Holy Communion interacts with the pastor who administers the sacrament and with all who receive it. The sacrament of Holy Communion moves the heart because Christ is present with us in this hour of worship. The sacrament touches the soul because the Holy Spirit is present as a redemptive force. It is the realization of the spiritual meaning expressed in Holy Communion that has kept alive and vital the faith and love that are in Christ Jesus our Lord.

From the earliest days of the Church, when Christians could find a suitable place, they gathered around the sacramental table. From the writings of the apostolic fathers, we are informed that, as they united in worship with the bread and wine, they were brought into the presence of the Spirit of the Lord Jesus. This has proven true of every Christian congregation that has served God with devout hearts and sincere faith. We pray that this may also be true of us.

That we worship in the presence and in the Spirit of our Lord, we ought never to doubt. It is in the awareness of this truth that our worship becomes meaningful. Our thoughts in prayer, hymns, and praise are turned away from the things of the world. Our minds and hearts are directed to the benevolence of God and to his mercy. The drama begins with the lighting of the candles, which signals the beginning of worship and the coming of God's Spirit to be with his people. The moments of silence are mystical, like the stilling of the elements as our awareness to spiritual things is heightened, and the stillness comes before the hearing of the still small voice. We seek to be in harmony with the aura of the service, to be at peace, and to be receptive to the word of the Lord. However much the message may be extended or illustrated, the elements are still the symbols of an atoning and saving Christ. We welcome the fact that the Lord is present with his people. His presence nurtures and sustains our faith in him.

The Drama of Holy Communion Witnesses Our Lord's Resurrection

There is a revelation of a mystery associated with the sacrament of Holy Communion. The evangelists tell us that a mystery has been revealed and made known to those who have turned to the Lord Jesus. Mark wrote in his gospel: "Unto you is given to know the mysteries of the kingdom of God" (Mark 4:11). Following in this train of thought, St. Paul wrote: "By revelation he hath made known unto me . . . the mystery . . . now revealed by the Spirit" (Eph. 3:3–5). A mystery is something that was unknown before, not as yet made manifest. It is that which may be profound or inexplicable because it needs the light of revelation. Revelation is always the giving of knowledge and understanding. Revelation reveals that which before was kept hidden. The apostle Paul said that it came by the Spirit, through which knowledge of the kingdom of heaven was given. When Mark wrote that to those who confessed Christ it had been given to know the mystery of the kingdom of God, he meant that they had been given spiritual perception and understanding.

When we say that we celebrate Holy Communion in the presence of a risen and living Savior, we bear witness to our Lord's resurrection. This too is part of the drama of Holy Communion. Had the new religious movement initiated by Christ ended with his body in a tomb, there never would have been our New Testament Christianity. The world would never have known the Christian faith that buried all the pagan gods that once occupied the devotion of Roman civilization. It was our Savior's cross and his resurrection that gave our religion its driving force. His sacrifice and conquering Spirit gave our faith its heroic nature and its eternal conquest over the human soul. We, the people of the church, come to the sacrament of Holy Communion because we have confessed Christ, because we know in whom we have believed. The strength of our religious life is founded in the certitude of our belief and the spiritual impulse of our soul. To us, this has been made known in the meaning of Holy Communion.

Behold, I show you a mystery: as often as we unite in worship, celebrate this sacrament, eat this bread and drink this cup, we bear witness to the power and wisdom of God. We acknowledge there are those who question, those who are uncertain, and still others who would like to believe fully. Yet, we are all made of a like nature. None of us is always a tower of strength composed like a structure of unbending steel. We are aware of the confessions: "my Faith is not too strong"; "I find it hard to believe certain things"; "so many things have happened and so many things have changed. Long ago, it must have been many ages ago, I may have believed like that."

I am not asking that we believe and accept a system of thought. I am asking that we remember the Lord Jesus Christ who loved us, who gave himself for us so that we can come to the table of sacrament in remembrance of him. I am asking that we remember Jesus Christ, of God the Son, who came from the threshold of heaven to seek and redeem our souls from destruction. We should be aware that he who would show us the Father, seeks to be present with us and to fill our being with the fullness of God. To those who inquired of our Lord about the meaning of life and existence, the Lord Jesus replied: "I am the resurrection and the life."

As often as we eat this bread and drink this cup we affirm our belief in the Savior's words. St. Paul, to whom was given the understanding of the mysteries of the kingdom, stressed that this concept, the resurrection of the Lord Jesus, was the center and foundation of all our believing in Christ. And taking the bread and wine into our bodies, we give testimony to our Lord. We may not comprehend all the mysteries of the kingdom of God, but this much has been revealed: that "God was in Christ reconciling the world unto himself" (2 Cor. 5:19). This is the table of reconciliation, the bread and wine of the new covenant and our eternal witness to the resurrection of the Lord Jesus Christ.

In the Drama of Our Lord's Supper We Affirm Our Belief in Immortality

> Behold, I show you a mystery; we shall not all sleep, but we shall be changed . . . and this mortal must put on immortality. (1 Cor. 15:51, 53)

In the confession of the Apostle's Creed, the Church universal declared:

> I believe in the Holy Catholic Church;
> I believe in the communion of saints;
> In the forgiveness of sins, and in the
> Resurrection of the body, and in the
> Life everlasting. Amen.

Simple words these. Actually, not too mysterious or incomprehensible: "communion of saints," "forgiveness of sins," "resurrection of the body," and "life everlasting." My daughter and my sons, when they were little, understood these words and believed them. Must we again, in our hearts, souls, and minds be as little children? Jesus thought so. A little child believes and embraces the Lord Jesus in his heart. A child imposes no bar to hold back the Spirit's entry to his soul. It was the reception of his grace and Spirit that our Savior desired to awaken in us, and this is the time and place of his appointing. With the Savior's gift of spiritual life comes the endowment of immortality. In receiving the bread and wine, we receive the Lord Jesus, and with him we receive life everlasting. Amen.

16

HOLY COMMUNION:
CREATIVE AND REDEMPTIVE

When he arrived in the city of Rome, St. Paul entered as a prisoner of the imperial government. This occurred even though the Roman official in the province in which he was accused had wished to release him. When the Jews objected to his release, the apostle felt compelled to make an appeal to Caesar. As a Roman and uncondemned, he exercised his right to appellate review. When questioned why he was bound, Paul replied: "For the hope of Israel I am bound with this chain" (Acts 28:20).

The consolation of Israel was for more than a prophet. It was for a Redeemer. All the promises of God made to the nation were bound up in the coming of the promised Messiah. Though he was confined in his movements, Paul's hope was a vibrant, vigorous expectation of his life's work and in the success of the Church of Jesus Christ. The sacrament of Holy Communion is expressive of the vibrant and vigorous reality for us. It is the pledge of the vindication of our trust in Christ. In this ceremony we are made aware that our expectations, as they are centered in Christ, for our loved ones, and for ourselves, can be realized. With faith, hope, and love, these redemptive desires are capable of fulfillment, and we must believe this: by hope we are saved.

Hope May Be Constrained

Doubt may possess us when our desires seem constrained, but then this is only an appearance, for hope is a feeling that what is wanted will happen. It is an expectation of good things. Paul's fetters were meant to restrain him, but they never restricted his outlook or his anticipation in the success of his mission. With us, worry, fear, and anxiety may become a drag that we permit to constrain all our dreams. We worry because we cannot see far enough ahead to be comfortable with the future. We acknowledge that the best-laid plans can go awry and falter, that we can be left without anticipated joy, and instead are burdened with the grief of loss. Yet this ought not to stop us from believing, hoping, and planning for the future. However varied our experiences, time is a moving stream, and we must still grapple with the issues of life.

All appearances to the contrary, the expectation of good things does not have to be curtailed or held in check. Clouds occasionally hang overhead because we think that there is some power apart from God that can block our way or some huge object that stands in our path. Actually, the things that we face or that may hinder our desires are not all that insurmountable. Though in prison and restricted in his personal movements, St. Paul still preached the Gospel. Yet, he confessed that he was bound in another way. Because of his belief in man, in justice, and in righteousness, he was held to his work by the love of God. He felt impelled to work for the reconciliation of the human race. The love of our Savior was a deep, strong, and abiding impulse in the heart of the apostle, and with such an earnest affection, no obstacle was insurmountable for him and it need not be for us. Holy Communion directs our thoughts to our faith in Christ Jesus, to the power of God, and to the grace of our Lord Jesus Christ. There is no power apart from God that can prohibit what he has proposed.

In Christ Hope Is Never Restrained

Paul wrote to the church in Colosse that, "Christ in you, [is] the hope of glory" (Col. 1:27). Reliance on God and on our Lord Jesus Christ is a strong, motivating force in the life of any individual. In our worship at the sacramental table, we experience the spiritual drama of our expectations for the future. After our Lord ascended to be with the Father, the Church was in need of a symbol to remind them that the reality of the Christian hope was of eternal significance. As a memorial for his people that this was so, Christ left them with the sacrament of Holy Communion, and it became for his followers an emblem of eternal hope. The Last Supper was a pledge for the Church that the spiritual power of faith in Christ could never be extinguished, by time, by adversity, or by the forces of evil. It is so even for us today. Our Lord, through the touch of his grace, can cause hope to spring eternal in the hearts of all his people.

If the Christian religion is to continue to have an uplifting and redemptive effect on our society, we must feel driven to do a great work. Our life and faith and our church are not so much what we did in the past, but what we are doing now. With a promise for the future, we can maintain vitality and work creatively in all our endeavors, because a thirst for life emerges from the desire to see some of our hopes realized. We must believe, if we believe anything at all, that the expectations that are centered in Christ for ourselves and his Church will be fulfilled. The anticipation of the good things that we have in Christ Jesus are like wings that lift us up when the let-down feelings come upon us. We can give expression to our religious nature and impulse. Individually, in a warring world, we can live at peace. In an unjust society, we can lead a good life. In the midst of all evasion, delusion, and unrighteousness, we can be honest, open, and righteous in all our acts. We would trust Christ to temper our spirits, and we pray for the time when the knowledge of our Savior shall cover the Earth. And yet, knowledge in itself is never enough. The Spirit of our Lord must be with us, his presence possess us, and his attitude of mind must be ours. In Christ our Lord, our hope is for victory, even over death itself.

Hope in Christ Is Creative and Redemptive

Good expectations are always creative and redemptive, even though for a time they may appear to have been constrained.

Michelangelo found his expression of life, which he desired to depict, in a garden of stone. Here were stones of all sizes, shapes, and colors. Others conceived these stones as discarded pieces of marble, but not so Michelangelo. As a sculptor, he saw faces and figures within each stone that he would release. In the energy of a God-given creative spirit, he transformed these pieces of marble into faces and figures of beauty. He moved among great contemporaries like Leonardo and Raphel. But in Michelangelo, the spiritual force, springing from the ideals and hopes of the Christian faith made him great. His creative spirit was impelled by men who walked in the way of the Lord and who expressed their hope for the human race.

While Christ in us is our hope of glory, it is Christ with us that is our hope of realization. In the cathedral of Orveito, Michelangelo saw, in the frescos, the illustration of the final destiny of man. The greatest impression he received was that of the majesty and glory of Christ as the creator and judge of all. Some years later, in his own painting, The Last Judgment, the central figure of Christ dominates the whole scene. We get the feeling that all who look to the person of the Lord Jesus Christ shall be redeemed out of all the turmoil going on in the world.

But for all those who have known the Lord Jesus, this redemption is much more than a mere impression, it is a cardinal reality of our faith. From all the turmoil that may surround our lives individually, from all the strife and distortions that may trouble the Church, from all its sufferings and loss, the Lord of the Church will surely redeem it and all she carries in her bosom. Our dreams and hopes, which may have appeared constrained like the beautiful faces and figures in the garden of stone, can be realized. In the sacrament of Holy Communion, our risen and living Lord has given us a pledge of his love, and his love causes hope to revive time and again in the human heart.

Within the beauty and simplicity of this sacrament, we are made aware that our Lord is present with us. He comes with his quickening Spirit to awaken all the dreams we have hid in our hearts. In this act of worship, our Lord's love and sacrifice are central, and if his love and grace are central in our lives, we are redeemed. As long as his presence is with us, this is all that really matters. In the words of an early church father:

> Seeing then that we have this hope, let us knit our souls to him who is ever true to his word and righteous in all his judgments. Amen. (Ignatius of Antioch, bishop of the Church in Syria)

17

JUDAS LEFT THE UPPER ROOM

The time for the Passover meal was drawing near and the Lord Jesus sent Peter and John to make preparations for the celebration of the ancient night of redemption. That was the night when the angel of death passed over the dwellings of Israel, and God had delivered his people from bondage. Having found an upper room, the disciples made ready. When the supper was completed and Jesus had explained the significance of the sacramental meal, he said: Behold, the hand of him who betrays me is with me on the table (Luke 22:21 RSV).

Judas Left the Upper Room

At the Last Supper, where the Lord Jesus instituted the sacrament of Holy Communion, he also signified Judas as the betrayer. Shortly thereafter, Judas Iscariot left the Upper Room to engage in his mission of betrayal, and what a tragedy his leaving that Upper Room revealed. When he sped off into the night, Judas turned his back on the promised Redeemer of his people, left the fellowship of the disciples, and separated himself from our Lord's mission of mercy. Iscariot surrendered all that was of spiritual value, because like Jezebel of old, he had sold himself to do evil in the sight of the Lord, and like Balaam, the son of Beor, when his way was perverse before the Lord, he had sold himself for gain. Unfortunately for Judas Iscariot there was no dumb ass endowed with human voice to restrain his madness: "For what shall it profit a man, if he shall gain the whole world, and lose his own soul?" (Mark 8:36).

Actually, Judas gained very little, only thirty pieces of silver, and despising the grace of our Lord Jesus Christ for personal gain, he lost his soul in the process. In his abrupt departure from the sacramental meal, Judas ran headlong into the realm of darkness and despair. The black of the eternal night had fallen on his soul. He suffered the loss of all expectation, separated himself from faith, hope, and love and from all the spiritual graces that accrue from our trust in the Lord Jesus.

Such has always occurred with those who turn away from this meek and gentle Savior of men and who turn from the grace of God. They have walked away from our Lord's forgiveness and absolution. And it is not really what one has gained, for no one will actually gain the whole world. Rather, it is the value of what one has lost. What is the real gain of it all if one has lost his soul? The man or woman who has lost his soul has lost all. For this supreme tragedy, the world has absolutely no compensation to offer. Judas had lost all, because some time previous to that night in the Upper Room, in his heart he had already rejected the Lord Jesus.

As many individuals like himself, Judas could not understand a Savior who would suffer for his people or a love that would lay down its life for a friend. He was unable to accept the fact that by his death the Lord Jesus would make many righteous. Service, sacrifice, and reconciliation were not germane to any mission conceived in the heart and mind of Judas Iscariot. He had hardened his heart against the kingdom of heaven, closed fast his soul against the influence of the Spirit, and had never turned to the Lord God with his whole heart or with any part of it.

Still, our faith is always a matter of the inner man, of a mind, soul, and spirit turned to God and to the grace of our Lord Jesus Christ. At the Last Supper, Jesus opened up his mind to the disciples, giving them insights to the things of the kingdom, and they knew that he would give himself for the life of the world. In the presence of the bread and wine, he had extended his life for all that claimed him as Savior and Lord. As we move into the sacramental service, we become aware that our Lord would lift the veil to the heavenly sanctuary as he did in that obscure Upper Room of long ago. Jesus offers us the gentle, yet strong, power of his Spirit to sustain us in our pilgrimage. He gives us his love and offers to redeem our soul, and this, all the physical power in the universe is unable to do.

Those Who Remained with the Lord Jesus

The Lord Jesus looked at the eleven who remained with him about the sacramental table and said:

> You are those who have continued with me in all my trials; and I have assigned you . . . a kingdom, that you may eat and drink at my table in my kingdom. (Luke 22:28–30)

The time of his departure had arrived and on the morrow the cross would be lifted up. Some of the disciples may have known what lay ahead. Perhaps Peter, James, and John, those of the inner circle who were closer to Jesus than the rest, may have known. But our Lord wanted all that were loyal to his cause to know that he had assigned them a kingdom. It was the kingdom of our Lord, one of Spirit, grace, and heavenly fellowship, and of the reign of God's Spirit in human hearts. In their service to the Master, the kingdom would be theirs to develop, nurture, and spread abroad. God had poured out his Spirit, and the people would live and know the Lord God, they would learn of the Lamb of God who takes away the sins of the world.

As ambassadors for Christ in their ministry, the disciples would not exercise lordship, but conduct themselves as meek saviors of men. They would be as those who serve, even as their Lord was among them as one who served. They would proclaim the Gospel of the kingdom, of God's grace, love, and long suffering with the children of men. While many had departed from the Way, those about the table had remained with the Lord Jesus. In the mystery of God's providence, it had been given unto them not only to believe on the Lord Jesus, but also to enter into the fellowship of the Savior's suffering. They were dedicated to the ministry of reconciliation.

The Passover meal was completed and the bread had been blessed, broken, and eaten. They had drunk from the cup, but would the disciples of our Lord be able to sustain that high spiritual intensity of their Savior's presence? Would they be able to continue to drink from his cup? Indeed, they would, for there is always a cross for all who serve. Each of the disciples was destined to suffer for the cause of Christ, but they would also glory that they were found worthy to have suffered for the name. As these men had remained with Jesus through all his trials, so they would continue faithful to his cause to the end of their days.

At Pentecost came the strengthening. The Spirit descended upon the Church of Jesus Christ in power, and the Gospel tide was impelled onward with ever-gathering force. From Jerusalem and all the cities of Judah, the Gospel tide rolled onward as the endless waves of the sea. The men of the kingdom ate and drank at the table of sacrament, for their Savior's presence enabled them to overcome the sufferings of the cup. As they continued in their work, they gave testimony to the grace of our Lord Jesus Christ.

We Who Share in the Sacrament

Our Savior has earnestly desired to eat his meal of the new covenant with us also, and he has assigned to us also his kingdom that we may eat and drink of the elements. It is Jesus who bids us do this in remembrance of him. Our Savior's one wish is that this be a true sacrament of inward and spiritual grace for our lives. In response to our having gathered here in faithfulness to his cause, he has come to be with us in his Spirit. Our Lord does not remain unmoved and indifferent to our needs of spirit and body while sitting at the right hand of God exalted.

As our souls awaken to the touch of grace, and as we partake of the bread and wine, we come to the height of our worship service. Looking to him with believing hearts, the body and blood of our Lord Jesus Christ will cleanse us from all unrighteousness.

Sharing in this sacrament, we are conscious that we share also in his suffering, that he took us to the cross with him, and that he granted to us there the remission of our sins, for our lives are hid of God in Jesus Christ. And having been buried with Jesus in baptism, we will also have risen with him in his resurrection. In sharing his Passover meal with us, Christ had made it the visible and continuing sign of his atonement. We will not be like Judas who left the Upper Room and fell into outer darkness, but like the disciples, we will continue always with our Lord. He in turn will continue to remain with us in all our personal trials.

For many, it may have already grown late, and the night is about to fall around them. It was toward evening when the Lord Jesus met the two disciples on the way to Emmaus. Their eyes did not recognize the Lord Jesus. But their spirits knew him, for their hearts were moved. Moving at the impulse of their hearts, the two disciples constrained the Lord Jesus, saying: "Abide with us: for it is toward evening, and the day is far spent" (Luke 24:29). The Lord Jesus stayed with them, and they knew him in the breaking of the bread.

The moment of the breaking of the bread is now. As we come to the sacrament of Holy Communion with faith, hope, and love, we can know the wonders of our Savior's grace. We will know that he comes to us in the bread and wine, and he would come to abide with us for all time. Though evening be near, the night will not fall around us, but the Lamb of God, which is in our midst shall be the light of our souls and the end of our faith, hope, and love. Amen.

18

THE MORNING STAR IN YOUR HEART

The memory is a strange and wonderful faculty. It is the mental ability of reproducing what one has learned or experienced in the past. More exactly, when the affections are moved, it involves the ability to recall an event in which we had a part and bring it to the foreground of consciousness. Memories can be quite effective when the images reproduced are sharp and clear, yet the years and preoccupation with many necessary things cause the images of past events to fade. There are many things about which we make a conscious effort not to forget, like our wedding day and its anniversary, the birth of our first child, and birthdays. Still, there have been occasions when even these significant events in our lives would have been overlooked had we not received adequate and pointed prompting.

In writing to the Christians scattered throughout the eastern provinces of the ancient Roman world, Simon Peter wrote in his second epistle:

> I intend always to remind you of these things, though you know them and are established in the truth. . . . I think it right that as long as I am in the body, to arouse you by way of reminder. (2 Peter 1:12, 13 RSV)

Peter wrote to the recipients to refresh their thoughts, to stir their mental images of past experiences in their religious lives. He wanted them to maintain the spiritual pulse of their souls. All the shades of meaning that our religion has for us are drawn from our past experiences, stored in our memory. The concept of our faith is made up of all our past and present religious encounters, of our prayers, confessions, our mental images of God and Jesus Christ, of the worship services we have attended, of the revival meetings and crusades we have been a part of, of the hymns and gospel songs we enjoy. Especially is our religious concept tempered by those moments when the Holy Spirit touched our hearts.

Why did St. Peter take time from his busy schedule to write to those who were already Christians and who knew the teachings of their faith well to remind them of these things? And why did he pledge to do so as long as he had breath?

The Need to Be Reminded

Simon Peter did so because he was aware of human nature. He knew that in his training for discipleship no one had failed the Lord Jesus and missed the mark as much as he. Is it not true that on the very night that Peter made his vow of eternal loyalty to the Lord Jesus, he denied his Master three times? Had he so soon forgotten? But he remembered when he heard the sound of the cock's crow. And when the Lord Jesus looked at him in the court of the high priest, he went out into the darkness of the night and wept bitterly. Peter wrote because he knew that in the realm of spiritual encounters and realities it was so easy to forget. No one goes about intentionally to disregard the importance of his religious life or deny his Lord. It is simply that other things keep crowding in, we get busy, neglect our personal devotional life, and we cease noticing the effect of this neglect. We are left with a passive faith because all the moving and compelling images have receded from the foreground of consciousness.

What do we remember about our first significant encounter with the Lord Jesus? Were we moved deeply? Were our minds drawn out to think about the meaning of existence? About God

and man, life, and death? Did we look to a saving and atoning
Christ? Is the impact of that encounter still vital to us? Was it a
transforming experience? Can we remember what we did immediately thereafter?

There is a component in personal computers called random ac-
cess memory. When the memory chips were first made, they were
thought to be a wonder because they could store about forty thousand bits of information. Then as development progressed, the chips
came to store four hundred thousand, and finally, over one million
bits of information. But being in the chip, the bits of information are
of no value unless recalled. They must be put to active use to be
effective. Our mental images of God the Father, the Lord Jesus Christ,
and the Holy Spirit should be brought into play when we worship,
read the scriptures, and pray. We must gather up the bits of our
religious experience and trust that we can conceive of our religious
life as a unified whole. Simon Peter wrote that, though the early
Christians knew these things and were well founded in the precepts
of their religion, he intended to continually remind them about those
things. Holy Communion seeks to move our hearts and awaken our
souls by stirring the religious images of our memory.

From the Table of Our Memory

Thomas More wrote:

Oft, in the stilly night
Ere Slumber's chain has bound me,
Fond Memories bring the light
Of other days around me.
(*Oft in the Stilly Night*)

The effectiveness of Simon Peter's work for the cause of Christ
occurred because he lived in the memory of his days of discipleship
with the Lord Jesus. He recalled how the Teacher come from God
spoke to the weary soul, healed the sick, and told stories about the
kingdom of heaven. Most of all, Simon Peter must have remembered how the Lord Jesus always came to his rescue, prayed for him,

warned him, instructed him, and loved him. These were fond memories of spiritual significance for him that brought the light of those happy days with the Lord Jesus around him. The memory of God's dealing with us in the past can do the same thing for us, sharpen the images, stir the heart, and nurture the life of the soul. After his departure, Peter wanted the saints to be able to recall these things, and this is one of the things that occurs with us when we celebrate the sacrament of the bread and wine. Holy Communion places our Lord's life and mission on the table of our memories and calls out the exercise of our faith. It brings the light of that eternal day around all that have united in worship with the elements of bread and wine.

Then, in his letter, Simon Peter told about the most moving hour of glory and grace that he had shared with his Lord, and as he wrote, he was recalling this event from the table of his memory:

For we did not follow cleverly devised myths when we made known to you the power and the coming of our Lord Jesus Christ, but we were eye witnesses of his majesty. For when he received honor and glory from God the Father and the voice was born to him by the Majestic glory, "This is my beloved Son, with whom I am well pleased," we heard the voice borne from heaven, for we were with him on that holy mountain. (2 Peter 1:16–18)

We ought not to allow the memory of our religious encounters to fade away, as a dream that recedes in the sleep of night and is gone in the morning. It really does not take all that much effort. A few moments of prayer, the memory of a meaningful passage of Scripture, and an expression of gratitude work effectively to this end. The strong spiritual force of Simon Peter's ministry, like the power of the coming of the Lord Jesus Christ, came in part from the memory of his experience when he was on that holy mountain with the Lord Jesus.

The Morning Star in Your Heart
Simon Peter added a bit more. He implied that keeping alive the memory of our past religious encounters had an additional

benefit. We need this additional benefit, because there are moments when all this seems far removed from reality, and there are
other times when, like the disciples in the garden, our souls are
heavy with sleep. It seems that we struggle to keep alive the sense
of the spirit in our lives, even though we sense that this ought not
to be so. Peter wrote:

> You will do well to pay attention to this as to a lamp shining in
> a dark place, until the day dawns and the morning star rises in
> your heart. (2 Peter 1:19)

That is a marvelous, redemptive thought; we are to remember
and think on these things, until the day dawns and the morning
star rises in our hearts. That is indeed a lovely evangel. It is like
that other promise of spiritual benefit when we celebrate the sacrament of Holy Communion, that we examine ourselves, and if we
are honest with ourselves and confess our need of grace and of our
Savior, he will be faithful and just to forgive our sins and to cleanse
us from all unrighteousness. Being attentive to these things, one
day, that moment will come. The time will come when we will no
longer have to struggle to be aware of our Savior's grace and love
residing in our hearts. Through one ineffable experience, the Holy
Spirit will give us the absolute certitude of the reality of our faith
in Christ Jesus. That touch of grace within us will never die out or
burn too low. It will become like a slow and steady warmth always
responding to the occasion of need. We will discover that, already,
the Spirit has made intercession.

In spite of what has occurred in the past, or what may occur in
the future, Holy Communion will always remind us of our faith in
Christ and in God the Father. We will believe that God "Knoweth
the way I take" (Job 23:10), and that all things work together for
good to those who love God and are called according to his purpose. We pray for grace to accept God's will and welcome the influence of the Spirit. Is this not his will, that we receive his Son
and keep alive the memory of his Passion? We do so when we
come to our Lord's table and witness to his love and sacrifice.

As the mental images are enhanced, our memory revives the spiritual experiences of the past, and, mingling with the present, our spiritual impulse is nurtured and strengthened. It can be as though, for us, the day had dawned and the morning star has risen in our hearts. The Bread of his Presence comes with the benediction of the Spirit, who renews the memory, clarifies the images, and gently touches the soul by way of reminder. Amen.

19

THE PRESENCE ENCOUNTERED

I n his Confessions, St. Augustine wrote:

How shall I find rest in thee, O Lord my God? and who will send thee into my heart? . . . Tell me of thy compassion, O Lord my God, what thou art to me. Say unto my soul, I am thy salvation. (St. Augustine, Confession)

Augustine expressed the universal desire of every man and woman who has ever sought a closer identity with the Lord God. How can we find rest for our souls? How can we find God? In the middle of our daily lives and all that they embody, can we even faintly hope to encounter the presence of the Eternal? In transforming the Passover meal into a sacrament of his kingdom, the Lord Jesus, as the new and living Way, assured us that he would meet with his people in the presence of God, and that we would know him in the breaking of the bread. In our minds and with our souls we may come into the presence of the Father of our spirits.

The Transformation

Therefore, if any one is in Christ, he is a new creation; and the old has passed away, behold, the new has come. All this is from

God, who through Christ reconciled us to himself. (2 Cor. 5:17, 18 RSV)

The birth of the sacrament of Holy Communion grew out of our Lord's desire to share the Passover meal with his disciples. Already, the twelve who had chosen to follow him were near the close of their discipleship. Good Friday would be the end of their direct instruction from the Lord Jesus. But their transformation, from those who sought their harvest in the sea, to men of the kingdom who would discharge their ministry of reconciliation, would not be completed until the coming of the Spirit on Pentecost. In the Upper Room, the disciples were in the process of growth, still learning about the mysteries of the kingdom. They watched and listened as Jesus of Nazareth, in his office of prophet and priest, drew the veil over the old as it passed away.

The Passover meal, which spoke of their redemption from bondage in Egypt, would henceforth speak about the remission of sins, absolution, the saving way of God's forgiveness, and the reconciliation of men and women to God the Father. The Lord Jesus told them plainly that the bread was his body broken and the wine his blood shed for the remission of sins. No longer would the harsh demands of the tablets of stone control the way God would deal with men or the way man might approach his presence. As it was always intended to be, the relationship between God and man, the Lord Jesus disclosed, was a spiritual fellowship, a matter of the heart and soul. God shed abroad his love in our hearts through the Holy Spirit that was given us, and his kingdom embodied the elements of peace and righteousness. Our communion with the Father came through faith in the Lord Jesus Christ. The two elements that were singled out from the Passover meal were the bread and wine, tokens of the body and blood of Christ. This was the meaning and the spiritual significance that Christ made, and that he gave to his disciples of the sacrament of Holy Communion, when first instituted. The Savior's thoughts and teaching pointed to the cross and the grave, which were but a few days away.

The transformation of the Passover meal, having been completed and made to embody more elevated spiritual teaching, was set before the disciples and the Church as the new and living way; and, "All this is from God, who through Christ reconciled us to himself." Holy Communion became the main sacrament of our Lord's kingdom, and in celebrating the sacrament, the Lord Jesus affirmed that we come into the presence of God in the unity of the Spirit.

The Presence Encountered

Athanasius, bishop of the sea of Alexandria, from his first exile, wrote to his people that, though they were separated by distance, they could keep their sacred feast together in the unity of the Spirit, because Christ united them. In the sacrament of the bread and wine we come face-to-face with great inner realities, with the presence that moves us in the wonder of elevated thoughts. Like the Savior in the Garden of Gethsemane seeking the nearness of God, from the depths of inner communion, we may emerge with new power to stand for Christ in the world at large. After the meal, the Lord Jesus, with three of his disciples, made his way to a garden on Mount Olive, which he used for prayer. In this quiet place, as he prayed, Christ sought closeness to God, renewal in the inner man, and resolution to do the Father's will. Because he came from the bosom of the Father, Christ always lived and worked in the aura of the presence of the Eternal Spirit.

Communion is sharing something with another, a mutual interchange of thoughts, and in the new and living way of Holy Communion; it is coming into the presence of the unseen God. We seek a mutual interchange of elevated thoughts, a feeling that we have come face-to-face with great inner realities that are good for the soul. In the Garden, from the depth of inner communion, Jesus expressed the thoughts that passed through his mind as he contemplated what lay ahead. He said, "Not my will, but thine be done." In his confession, Christ identified himself with the purpose of God:

For it is God who said, "Let light shine in darkness," who has shone in our hearts to give the light of the knowledge of the glory of God in the face of Christ. (2 Cor. 4:6)

What was the purpose of God having shed abroad his spirit in our hearts? It was to give us the knowledge of his presence in Jesus Christ, the spiritual perception to understand this and the appreciation to receive it and make it our own.

How shall we find the presence of God? And how shall we find rest for our souls? We find God's presence in his Son, Christ our Lord, in the worship service, in the celebration of the bread and wine, and in the immanence of the Holy Spirit. We sense the Spirit in the mystery of great inner realities and through the moments of deep communion. We find rest for our souls in the saving way of God's forgiveness, in reliance upon his grace embodied in the consecrated bread and wine, and in turning our hearts and thoughts to the Lord Jesus. But we must meet him who is the glory of God, who is the fullness of God, and who is the expressed image of his person. We must meet him who carries the image of the Passover meal, the heart of its significance, the day and night of redemption. Though we may know him as the Son who brought the knowledge of God and his kingdom, we must know him in his office of reconciliation. In the elements of bread and wine he comes to us as our Redeemer.

Treasure in Our Earthen Vessels

But we have this treasure in earthen vessels, to show that the transcendent power belongs to God. (2 Cor. 4:7 RSV)

When St. Peter wrote "all this is from God," he meant that this was the way of God's appointing, who gave us the revelation of himself in the presence of the Lord Jesus Christ. God has touched us in our inner nature with his grace. We carry about in our earthen vessels our experience with the Lord Jesus. We carry with us the knowledge that we have of him, the inner impulse of our souls—

our feelings, sensations, and thoughts with the residence of the Spirit. Though our bodies may be subject to illness, death, and decay in our cycle of life, the transcendent power and source of our religion lie with God. Since all this is of God, and this is the way of his appointing, he will receive us as we unite in the celebration of this sacrament in a fellowship of believers.

As we look to him who has created us in his image, and who created all the worlds around us, Holy Communion can be for us the moment of our personal encounter with the Lord Jesus. Our fellowship is with the Son and with the Father. His presence with us is to assure his people of the continuity of his love and of his ministry of reconciliation. The Savior comes as our personal Redeemer to revive our spirits and encourage our faith in him. We can take the bread and wine into our bodies, just as we are. Because we do so at his invitation, he will receive us, and because he always has the words of eternal life, he will draw near us. In coming to the bread and wine of Holy Communion, we come to the throne of grace. In the Bread of his Presence we have come to Mount Zion, to the city of the living God, "and to Jesus Christ the mediator of the new covenant" (Heb. 12:24). Amen.

20

RESPONDING TO THE PRESENCE

One of the greatest things in life is the knowledge of God whom to know aright is eternal life. We know God supremely as he is manifested in Christ our Savior. And though we may not be aware of it, God's presence is all about us, for in the last analysis, it is him in whom we live, and move, and have our being. In opening our lives to our Savior's influence, our deepest destiny is fulfilled. But this can never be done unless we acknowledge his presence, and we can do so whenever we celebrate the sacrament of Holy Communion. To experience in our own lives the spiritual depth of our faith, we must respond to our Lord's love and grace. When we partake of the consecrated elements of bread and wine, it can be for us an hour of mystic, sweet communion with Father, Spirit, and Son.

The Scriptures characterized King David as a "man after God's own heart." It was not because David, either as a shepherd boy or king, was any more righteous or holy than others. In fact, many times he was not. But it was because David responded to God's presence and influence, and he did so with heart and soul. There was in David a willing surrender to the influence of the Holy Spirit and submission to the will of God. This attitude expressed his deep faith and reliance on the Lord God. When the Holy Spirit moved in David, he felt compelled to give expression to his thoughts in his Psalms. It was as though the joy of his spiritual communion with God overflowed for him in the same faith and love that is ours in Christ Jesus. David wrote:

> I love the Lord, because he hath heard my voice and my suppli-cations. Because he has inclined his ear unto me, therefore will I call on him as long as I live . . . Gracious is the Lord, and righteous; yea, our God is merciful. The Lord preserveth the simple: I was brought low, and he helped me. Return unto thy rest, O my soul; for the Lord hath dealt bountifully with thee. (Ps. 116:1–7)

God Desires Our Response

Our Lord Christ Jesus seeks to awaken our souls to the touch of his grace. God, as the Father of all, desires an awareness of his presence from his people. Our redemption is still an unfinished product, and it is also an ongoing process. As unfinished, we do not yet measure up to the fullness of Christ, and until we respond, we can never be made whole. This is not only true of our spiritual lives, it is also true of all our natural abilities and aspirations. "God created man in his own image, in the image of God created he him; male and female created he them" (Gen. 1:17). He has crowned us "with glory and honor," and has given us dominion over the works of his hand. Human beings can evolve and mature and they can be creative in their own right. Every man or woman has many possi-bilities within him or her. But most are like an unfinished sym-phony. One of the major works of Schubert, a symphony in B minor was written and left unfinished for some time. It is called "The Unfinished Symphony." When finally made public and played, it echoed time and time again with beautiful music and harmony.

Until he responds to the love and grace of God manifested in Christ Jesus, man as he was meant to be is not in harmony with his Creator. His internal life—the mind, spirit, and soul—are filled with stress and discord. But let him awaken to God's love and grace and his life can be made whole. Man's life can be harmonized and put in tune with God and spiritual realities. God put his love in our hearts through the Holy Spirit, and our response is something that we do in answer to the manifestation of his Spirit in our lives.

Thus it was that David prayed: "I love the Lord, because he has heard my voice and supplications. Because he has inclined his ear to me, therefore will I call on him as long as I live." We assent to the truth of David's words and pray with him: "Return, O my soul, unto your rest; for the Lord has dealt bountifully with you." Sharing in this sacrament of the bread and wine can be our golden moment. As we partake of the elements that symbolize our Savior's love and sacrifice for us, we witness with faith, hope, and love. We can display a willing surrender to the influence of the Holy Spirit in our lives.

Response, a Religious Experience

One day when the crowds were beginning to drift away from Jesus in large numbers, our Lord turned to the disciples and said, "Will you also go away?" Answering for the twelve, Simon Peter replied immediately, "Lord, to whom shall we go? thou hast the words of eternal life" (John 6:68). Whenever he was near the Lord, Peter reacted to the presence of Christ and his faith grew by these experiences. Generally, our faith is a religious experience. It is something that our soul has gone through, and we must have been touched by the Savior's grace because our spiritual life comes from Lord Jesus. Our faith as a religious experience must come from our union with Christ Jesus. The awakening of the mind and soul comes from the revelation of God's grace within us. Our heart and mind must say to us, "I know that he is my Savior-God. I know that it is he who has made heaven and Earth and redeemed my soul from destruction." As a religious expression, our faith means that we believe in God and trust in him. And the Holy Spirit, which is given us, brings the confirmation of God's existence and presence.

Having been touched by his grace, we come to love Christ because our Lord undertook our cause upon himself and discharged our obligations on the cross. He made us his. In worship and prayer, the thoughts of our hearts ascend to God. We receive, accept, and rest on our Savior's promises. This response can be a never-ending experience in our religious lives, for:

> Gracious is the Lord, and righteous; our God is merciful. The Lord preserves the simple; when I was brought low, he saved me. Return, O my soul, unto your rest: for the Lord has dealt bountifully with thee.

The Response Springs from the Heart

The appeal of the Gospel comes from a subtle sympathy of soul to soul, and each must be in touch with God if we are to know him through our own personal encounter. There must be impressed in our minds a vision and a sense of God that we have gained through our own religious growth. Having obtained this vision and sense of God, we accept it as true because we have felt it in our hearts and acknowledged it in our minds. When we look to God in worship, the Spirit stirs the impulse of our soul as the Holy Spirit comes to us with gentle love and overwhelming power—bringing us the renewal of spiritual life, certainty, and peace. As we surrender to the will of God, the presence of our Lord transforms and renews the whole of man.

Ultimately, a true yearning must come from within us. It is a heart turning to God in our Lord Jesus Christ. His coming was an invitation for us to enter his kingdom, and the touch of the Spirit prompts our response.

When asked whether he loved Jesus, Peter replied, "Lord, thou knowest I love thee" (John 21:15). Our Savior had asked him three times, and on each occasion Simon Peter affirmed his love and loyalty to Christ. If the Savior were to ask the same question of us, "Lovest thou me?" I am sure that he would expect a reply. As an expression of our love, it would be one of faith and trust in him. Most of all, he would want us to acknowledge him as Savior and Lord. As we make ready to take into our bodies the bread and wine of Holy Communion, let us also make ourselves ready to be receptive of his grace. As we do this in memory of him, the Spirit will restore our souls, and we will move closer to his fullness. Christ alone can make us whole and harmonize our lives with spiritual realities. To know Jesus as he really is, we respond to him with heart, soul, and mind; and no longer need we guess or doubt, for Christ will make himself known.

He that loveth me shall be loved by my Father, and I shall love him, and will manifest myself to him. (John 14:21)

Amen.

To order additional copies of

Have your credit card ready and call

Toll free: (877) 421-READ (7323)

or send $9.99** each plus $4.95 S&H* to

WinePress Publishing
PO Box 428
Enumclaw, WA 98022

www.winepresspub.com

**WA residents, add 8.4% sales tax

*add $1.00 S&H for each additional book ordered